Dear

Bumbling Boy...

An author's assessment: Turning online dating blunders into creative characters

by *Jenny Dee*

Dear Bumbling Boy...

©2023 by Jennifer Dee Communications LLC

Cover Artwork Elements ©2023 Katja Frischbutter/Depositphotos.com, Iuliia Shevchenko/Depositphotos.com, Nadezhda Snopek/Depositphotos.com, Vladimir Zadvinskiy/Depositphotos.com

Print ISBN: 978-1-954687-13-4
Ebook ISBN: 978-1-954687-14-1

Printed in the United States of America

Dedication

To all my single friends...
One day our prince will come.
Until then, let's just laugh
at all the frogs we're forced to kiss.

Foreword

I connected with Jenny years ago—not surprisingly through my dating website. Jenny's sharp wit, impeccable timing, and silly side caught my attention, and we commiserated over the anguish of navigating the hunt for partnership.

It is hard not to appreciate a person who can make experiences that might traumatize a softer soul into a funny story that educates the rest of us, so of course, we became friends. There is not much I admire more than another kick-ass chick who gets things done while simultaneously raising children as a single parent and still following her dreams. We have appeared together on online shows, and she never fails to impress me with her wisdom while cracking me up.

Who doesn't know multiple attractive, kind, powerful, and witty women who remain single despite their charm?

Jenny is one of these women and has a uniquely self-aware affinity for recognizing both sides in each situation, as evident in this clever book about her online dating experiences. She is able to relay her stories in a lighthearted way that takes responsibility for her own insecurities without letting any of these guys off the hook for their actions and behaviors.

All of these stories made me laugh as I cringed at the similarities in my own dating history. I, too, have been stood up, annoyed, embarrassed, fascinated, amused, and everything in between on dozens of dates I had high hopes for. The struggle is real, and though I wish no one else ever had to go through it, the ugly truth is that a little (okay BIG) part of me is glad it wasn't just me.

Dear Bumbling Boy...

Sometimes all it took to give me the courage to get back out there and try again was the knowledge that others were on a similar journey. Luckily, I no longer need to suffer through such anguish, as I have a wonderful husband who was worth the wait.

If you are stuck trying to navigate the starts and stops of new relationships, then this is the book that will help you laugh through the chaos of modern-day dating. It probably isn't going to give you all of the answers that Cupid could (and if you find that sucker, let him know I would like to have a word with him!), but it will make your heart a little lighter as you go.

Maybe all you need to carry on in your hunt for partnership is to laugh while you remember that you are not really alone in your journey! ♥

Hilary Ritter (Young)
Founder of AstrologyDating.com*

* Note: this site was retired after Hilary found her happily ever after

Introduction

Online dating. What can I say about it?

It sucks.

It's an awful means to an end that has eradicated the beauty of traditional meet-cutes. Gone are the days of bumping into a soulmate randomly in a Blockbuster and swooning instantly over his (or her) eyes and smile while you reach for the same vintage VHS tape.

Now, we all get to cull through filtered photographic misinterpretations just to awkwardly await the infamous results: will it be the unsolicited profanity pic, the blatant 'let's meet up and have last-name-less sex,' or, my personal favorite, 'let's match then ghost.'

Let's explore these, shall we?

The desire to send dick pics. Pray tell, gentlemen… Why the hell would I want to see a pinup of your penis? Seriously?

First of all, I already don't know if your face is even going to be real, and you expect me to get excited over a conveniently angled mugshot of your lower brain? Second of all, unless your member can actually hold a conversation more intelligently than your upper brain, I don't want to engage it.

Lastly, a still picture of a random erection does nothing for me personally. I don't run out to buy porn magazines for dick visuals to masturbate to. So no, I do not want to see OR SEND pictures of our privates, especially before we have even met.

Not judging women who are into it, by the way (are there any?). However, based on the number of women I actually know and talk to, not a single one of us welcomes the moment when an unexpected cock appears on our phone screen.

Now, if you want to send a pic of you dressed up like a naughty Captain Jack Sparrow? Let's talk.

And speaking of pictures... Can we stop using words like catfish and fatfish, when you're holding an actual picture of a fish that is just as repulsive as your physical expectations? Hold up the last book you read. That would be impressive. What's not impressive is saying you went to the school of hard knocks. We all have. Find some originality, dude.

Sorry. I do have this tendency to tangent at times. Why am I single? Haha. Anyway...

Next: the 'let's just meet up and have sex' matches. Here's my problem with this one: you are basically telling me that you KNOW from a PICTURE or two that we are going to have enough physical chemistry to want to fuck upon meeting? In what universe?

Yes, I understand that there are men and women just looking to get laid and that this interaction is common. Again, not judging the mutually-reciprocated desires. My point is: when this intention is mixed within the same atmosphere of real dating interest, it's no wonder that no one can ever find what they are truly looking for on either side of the spectrum. Hookups find relationship-seekers, and LTRs find FWBs.

Maybe if people actually *read* the profiles or were *honest* on them, they would realistically match with what they were looking for without surprises or false expectations.

But I digress—there are way too many variations of dating I could get into here but won't. The perspective I am diving into in this book is actually one of intentional dating and not straight-up sex—though, as you will see, I have had my share of diverse intentions as this process ebbed and flowed. I haven't been all goody-two-shoes the whole time, but I've learned a lot about personal limits and expectations along the way.

Back to my picture pondering. I get that we are gauging potential attraction based on mere pictures, and for some of us (ME), what we read in the profiles also contributes to the interest factor. (Yes, I read them. I actually, truthfully read them.) As a sapiosexual, I will admit that a man's choice of words can further the attraction behind the scenes.

But am I going to predict whether I will find you (or expect you to find *me*) appealing enough to dive right in? Hell, no.

Traditional one-night stands work well because the in-person spark is the chemistry catalyst that catapults us into the immediate rush of sex (even under beer-goggle circumstances). Planning it based on an online interaction does NOT have the same effect. Trust me: we ALL look different in 3D, and our energy vibes do not always match the 2D.

So if you are online looking for a guaranteed one-night stand, at least from me, I'm gonna have to pass because those opportunities are reserved for the impromptu, out-of-town, charming millennial bartenders who give me just the right amount of free alcohol.

Sorry, not sorry, but this online dating chick does require an investment of at least a decent dinner or an outing in which we can get to know each other better first. I'm sorry, not sorry, if your past experiences have been with women who are only looking to get meals for free... but that doesn't give you the right to deny *me* an actual date before attempting to get in my pants. I ain't free... but I'm generous when treated right and feeling right.

Think of the song from Chicago the Musical: "When you're good to mama, mama's good to you."

So no, I'm not automatically going to decide from an online picture and profile that I'm just gonna meet up and give it to you. I don't even know if you have any manners, how you smell, or if you can manage to talk both clean and dirty to my satisfaction. And I can tell you this: if you start out being sexual without trying to get to know me in any way, you're not going to make it 24 hours.

Being high maintenance and having high standards are two completely different things.

Finally: the ghosting thing. I'm not talking about the "hey, we matched, but I changed my mind, and we unmatched without really pursuing anything" disappearance. I think that's, unfortunately, a normalized occurrence these days. With so many fish out there, we can't apologize for every erroneous net cast.

I'm talking about having a reasonable exchange of conversation—sometimes all text, sometimes moved to a phone call, sometimes a date is planned—and then out of nowhere, poof the magic dragon, they're gone. How is that mature?

Are we really all that scared of truth and honesty that we can't simply say something like, I'm not feeling the connection, or I met someone else, or I realized you are too amazing a woman to drag into my uncommittable world of unhealed emotional hell? Is that too much to ask for?

Come on, people. Let's not lie and say we do it because it spares someone's feelings. It doesn't. It spares **us** from the guilt of rejecting someone, and that's so cowardly and shows poor character (and creates bad karma, no thanks!)

Ghosting is a lot more hurtful than simply being real. I can tell you with a 98% return rate that every single time I have had the courtesy to reach out and be honest with a man and gently tell him I was unmatching or not interested in pursuing, he was grateful and always replied with an equally kind message thanking me and/or wishing me well also. Even fly-by online connections can be handled with everyday common decency.

We are all people with feelings behind these screens, no matter what confidence or mask we project.

Continuing on… I'm sure most online daters are familiar with those classic scenarios. Or sometimes you'll get the endless pen pal who avoids actually meeting up. Or a person who claims they want deep, personal connection and conversations but answers with one word and no follow-up.

Or someone so eager to meet up that you can smell the red flag love-bombing narcissist or scammer looking for your bank account transfer from a mile away (Hi, "Joel!").

Occasionally, a few slip through the cracks, and you make it to a first date, and that's a whole other slew of interesting ridiculousness I'm not going to get into now (you'll see some doozies as we get into the book instead). Sometimes, you even find a good egg to spend time with and get to know, and then it either progresses or doesn't.

Let's avoid the natural (and quite possible) assumption that it really is *me* that's the issue. You may even be reading this and shaking your head, *not* wondering why I haven't had too much dating success.

Passing on that realistic thought, what the fuck is wrong with people out there? Dating should not be this impossible shitshow.

We've been desensitized to human emotions and forget that our sole purpose in all of this is for connection, even those seeking purely sexual experiences. Y'all still want to feel a connection (I'll spare you the psychology behind it, but trust me, there is meaning in the meaningless).

So, why are we taking a platform intended for connection and wrecking the hell out of it? And this is happening on all sides of the sexual spectrum, no matter your gender identification or orientation (I'm quite sure if I dug in further, I'd find the LGBTQ+ dating world experiencing similar frustrations).

This book is written about my experiences dating heterosexual men, but from what a majority of what some men have told me about WOMEN—what the actual fuck, ladies?

Why are we using men to see how much money we can get from them? Why are we playing chasing games and emasculating them to the point where they have no desire to court the modern-day female? Why are we sending pussy pics and cultivating a culture of disrespect?

Now, that's not me being a prude or anti-sexual or even all that judgmental (okay, maybe a little), but come on. If y'all are into sharing pics, do your thing… but at least wait until you meet the guy before putting your offer out on the internet for big brother to access and use for his own pleasure at any time. Think before you press send!

Alrighty, I'm stepping off my soapbox. I am clearly by no means qualified to judge anyone and am far from perfect, as I am acutely aware of my own dating psychosis. You will certainly see it for yourself!

This book was actually written as a means to lighten up my own dating disappointment and bring humor instead of frustration to the countless souls out there who are nodding their heads and mumbling, "Amen, sister."

The idea came to me after one particular date happened while taking a class about creating characters for books. It dawned on me that these bumbling dating interactions were mere research opportunities for characters in upcoming novels that I'd write. Physical traits, personalities, backgrounds, different cultures, and even things said in conversation became literary ammunition (in both good and comical ways).

And to set the record straight, this is based on experiences on multiple date sites, so I am not advocating for or against any site in particular. Each one serves its purpose and is successful in its own right for a reason.

This is solely my personal (in)experience in the world of online dating and how I amuse myself by turning failures into fictitious potential.

Dear Bumbling Boy...

Thank you for indulging my sarcastic wit as I conduct an author assessment that connects my personal life to character development. I am not a man-hater, and this is not an attempt to belittle the men I have interacted with. It's all done tongue-in-cheek, and they are pretty much unidentifiable, with real names being completely omitted.

What I did not change, however, were the mind-baffling one-liners that came from so many of them. Oh no—those are too pure gold not to include verbatim.

So, sit back and enjoy the character profiling. It's gonna get sassy in here.

Cheers,

Jenny

The Men

HOW DATES TURN INTO FUTURE BOOK CHARACTERS

What does your character do to show his personality?

(A) Confirmed he was a friendly ghost...TOO friendly.

(B) Delivers witty flirtations as only a wordsmith can.

(C) Does have a good sense of humor.

What does your character look like on the outside?

(A) More ancient like a ghost than expected, with a really weird, long Santa beard.

(B) Did look good in a black leather jacket & jeans, so let's just trim some beard and salt and pepper him to make him more youthful.

Name:
Casper

What does your character say to show his personality?

"What's your bra size? I'm respectfully asking, of course."

Character Assigned:
The guy who gives you the shovel to bury the accidental dead body.

What lesson does your character bring about in your story?

That it's okay to ghost a ghost or unfriend the too-friendly.

Artwork Credit: Кирилл Кулаков/Depositphotos.com

Casper the Too-Friendly Ghost

$\triangleleft \quad \quad \quad \quad \quad \quad \heartsuit \quad \quad \quad \quad \quad \quad \triangleright$

How Far Did He Make It?
One Date

The Backstory:

I thought he had an interesting, older man, debonair-like look, but more than that, I could tell from his profile that he knew how to use words properly. I was right—he dabbled with being an author and enjoyed writing erotica novels (my first clue). The irony has not been lost on me that the writer who literally tried to encourage me to meet him for "research" ended up being my very first character assessment.

Well played, universe.

Anyway, he tried to insist that we just meet up for said "research," but I skillfully coerced him into agreeing to a simple drink first. I made it clear that he would not have access to my literary-inspired resources, but if he really was all that interested in me, he would take the risk and man up.

So, why would I want to meet up with him knowing he really only had one intention in mind? Believe it or not, beyond his sexual idiosyncrasies, he actually was a pretty cool conversationalist, and I'm a complete sucker for engaging wordsmiths. My core love language is words of affirmation, after all.

Well, when we finally met up at a bar, he was a lot older than I expected—and just as dirty-minded as he promised. He was very touchy with his hands and suggestive with his mouth. And so, after having that drink, I bid him good night, and off we went on our separate ghostly ways. But not before I got some pretty good material to make the character profiling pic that began this sarcastic book compilation of online dating encounters. (Thank you, Casp!)

Classic Line(s):

"It's my policy not to meet for drinks or dinner."

[It's my policy not to just put out.]

"What's your bra size? I'm respectfully asking, of course."

[Of course! I'm happy to share my intimate details with a complete stranger... Not.]

"Wouldn't you like some really good research for your romance novels? I could show you things you'd blush writing about."

[I'm pretty sure I've already written stuff I could make YOU blush about... but a clever flirting tactic. Still... HARD pass.]

Future Character Attributes:

He did have a cynical sense of humor and looked oddly good in a black leather jacket and jeans for his age and persona. I could just trim some beard and salt and pepper him instead of portraying the full-on gray to adapt him into a younger character.

Role I Would Assign Him:

He could prove to be an amusing side character, like the guy who gives you the shovel to bury the accidental dead body.

My Takeaway:

That it's okay to ghost a ghost or unfriend the too-friendly.♥

The Secret Agent Scammer

How Far Did He Make It?

Texting

The Backstory:

This guy was HOTTTT—which should have been my first inkling that something was up. At first, he seemed to speak quite well and was very interesting. We exchanged numbers, and little by little, the tone became conversationally weird with tons of bad grammar and "fa shos." But we never spoke; it was always text.

Why, you ask? Because he was a "secret agent," and he wasn't allowed to use his phone for calling. However, once I got "clearance," I'd be added to the list of people (like his mom) who would be authorized to call.

It was alarming and amusing all at once. I was thinking, if you really were a secret agent, you wouldn't be telling me that. But green on the dating scene as I was, I allowed it for a bit. That is, until one conversation had me taken aback and made me aware of a huge red flag: how he couldn't wait to get me and the kids all alone on a vacation where no one could bother us and we could really get to know each other better.

Follow that up with a convo with my very online-savvy girlfriend, who instructed me on how to use Google reverse images, and voila! My secret agent was none other than some poor guy who has repeatedly been the victim of countless dating photo scams. Needless to say, I called "Joel" out so that he knew I was on to him, and peace out it was… but not before

I indulged in a few more ridiculous chats about his secret agent work for shits and giggles on my part.

Classic Line(s):

"Your smile captures my heart and soul."

[I swooned at the time.]

"Guess we're lucky to have found each other's. Fa sho."

[Uh-oh. Not sure I can handle his lack of grammar and poor punctuation skills.]

"I can't wait to take you and the kids away on vacation where no one can bother us."

[Um... WHAT? Pass me the red flag, please.]

Future Character Attributes:

There were definitely some interesting stories and secret agent "intel" I potentially gathered, from clearance issues and communication restrictions to clandestine meetings and so on. How it ended with him being a scammer was also a pretty cool way of setting up a character to be "too good to be true" and then have him turn out to be a serial killer or something equally disturbing.

Role I Would Assign Him:

Listen, who wouldn't love a secret agent lead male in a romance? Except legit. Or, a secret scamming psycho. This guy gave me lots of good character ammo, fa sho!

My Takeaway:

If he's too insanely good-looking and interested to be true, he's a bot. ♥

The Off-Hours Responder

<hr>

How Far Did He Make It?

One Date

The Backstory:

This was definitely a different kind of experience—impulsive for me, even. We had matched and chatted a little bit before deciding to get back to each other on some possible days to meet up. I then excused myself for the night to go watch a movie with my son, but then my son decided he was going to go out with friends instead. My daughter was also out and about… so that meant I had three hours to myself on a Saturday night. And for some unusual reason, I didn't want to hermit those three hours away in a book like normal.

Since he was local, I was open to the idea of going on a date sooner than later and thought, *'What the hell? Why not?'*

So I did the unexpected and messaged him about my change of plans and asked if he wanted to meet up for coffee. He did! So within the hour, we found a Barnes and Noble open that had a Starbucks inside to meet up at. When he walked in, I was taken by surprise. I think I was expecting some short weirdo dork, but the man who walked in was tall, wide (not big, just broad), and handsome. While he had more of a boy-next-door kind of look, I couldn't help but think he was really attractive with kind eyes.

We grabbed coffee and tea, had a really great conversation, and then sat outside for a bit when the store closed until my son texted for a ride home. He seemed to be a pretty sensible and caring dad, a responsible worker, and had a great attitude about building a life for enjoyment at our age. I had a lot of respect for his viewpoints, even though I got the hint that we weren't aligned on some values—but at that point, it wasn't a dealbreaker.

I recognize there are shades of gray in perspectives, so as long as someone isn't offensive or obnoxious about what they believe in, I have no issue with respectfully disagreeing.

Anyway, he didn't try to make any moves, but I actually didn't mind that. I enjoyed his company, and we left off by saying that we'd meet up again. Well… that actually never happened. We had a second date for bowling planned, but at the last minute, he had to cancel because he was caught up at work. Then he never rescheduled, became distant, and only texted at like four in the morning before work when he knew I was sleeping. Finally, I decided not to wait around for a second date that wasn't going to come.

Classic Line(s):

"I've worked hard all my life. Now, I have a life and a schedule that allows me to enjoy life. I just have to remember to do that instead of using my free time to keep helping everyone else out."

[Here! Here!]

"Never mind—I'm not making a wager. I bet you're hustling me. You have your own ball and shoes just waiting to kick my ass, don't you?"

[His cute response to placing a bet about who would win at bowling—a date that never happened, anyway.]

Future Character Attributes:

There was something sexy about his blue-collar job aspirations and overall masculinity that screamed leading male character. He had a subtle manliness that wasn't all alpha or in your face, but still, you could tell he was a man's man.

Role I Would Assign Him:

I could use part of his masculine energy as part of a leading character. That's about it, though.

My Takeaway:

You never know what to expect—so even those guys with meh pictures might turn out to be someone you find extremely attractive in person, not just physically but mentally and emotionally. Allow yourself to indulge in surprises.♥

The Eastern European Boss

---❦---

How Far Did He Make It?
Phone Call

The Backstory:
I will admit the whole European thing had me intrigued. The culture, the suave nature, his accent—all of it enough to be swoon-worthy. We chatted on and off for a bit, usually in between respective work breaks. I didn't get much of a chance to learn about him before he threw on the long-term commitment expectation, and we hadn't even met or planned to meet at that point yet.

Now, I'm not one to move at turtle speed, but even *I* know to at least have a date or plenty before seeking a commitment. Yikes! I bailed rather quickly.

Classic Line(s):
"I feel like it will be best if you give it a break for now and focus with me just as I have done so we can see what the future holds. Hope I am not asking for too much on that?"

[Well, we haven't even met yet… so uh, yeah.]

Future Character Attributes:
I most certainly adored the European sophistication and entrepreneurial vibe he gave off, along with the sexy accent.

Role I Would Assign Him:

He might have to be the "tempter," someone who comes along to try to steal away the ingenue's affections but turns out not to be what she expected, throwing her back into the arms of the man she truly loves. Or something like that.

My Takeaway:

Not to assume a sexy accent will lead to a fantasy relationship with a "foreigner," as if I was traveling through Tuscany on vacation.♥

VALUABLE LESSONS TO LEARN
ACCORDING TO AN MBA ALL-STAR

- Regular store cinnamon is toxic; buy ceylon cinnamon for maximum health benefits.

- I don't have the right student loan to qualify for federal forgiveness.

- I need to be a little more mindful of my money, like shop in bulk at Costco.

- Disney no longer sells annual passes in its scheme to rip locals off.

- If I want a sugardaddy, then I just have to dress up and go to the Del Mar races.

- If I want to have sex with Johnny Depp, I can't brag about it because I have to sign an NDA first.

- My landlord would benefit from me installing an EV charging station in the garage for the next car I will buy, which will need to be electric.

The Political Money-Saver

How Far Did He Make It?

Multiple Phone Calls

The Backstory:

This guy was an interesting cat. He was super smart—all the way up to an MBA with long-term career goals that he was actively pursuing. He was also a great conversationalist and would probably make a killing on a trivia show with all the information and facts he had stored in that brain of his.

Sometimes it became a little much, like when he crossed the line to talk too much about politics, but I have to say, he wasn't disrespectful about his politics. He'd state his opinion, how it affected him, and lend some interesting facts or stories to back it up, and oddly enough, I found those stories enlightening. I'm apolitical myself, but the things he was saying seemed to align mostly with what I go along with, so I allowed it.

He also had a way of being financially responsible and super knowledgeable about all kinds of legal, tax, and bargain matters—which I typically find boring, but again, his wisdom certainly made our conversations enlightening. I also learned the difference between certain cinnamons, celebrity sex NDAs, the backstory of Disney annual passes, and a whole slew of other topics.

The only thing is, he would do all of the talking, and that made me feel dumb, like I didn't have much to contribute. I'm not all that worldly, so I was certainly getting an education. But he was a lover of Disney and all things theme park-related, and we're both business savvy, so we found enough common ground to be engaging with each other. And he was consistent in his communication—not too much, but he didn't flake out either. I thought I was going to like him when we got the chance to meet.

But we weren't meant to meet. He had just sold his car due to his expectation of the economy imploding and was in transportation limbo as his new car wasn't due to come in for another month. So I offered to drive to him and do something locally to his area, but he never made an effort back for a plan.

I ultimately decided that it wasn't worth my time to coordinate a lukewarm date and sent him a brief note to close out the connection, which was very cordially reciprocated. Nice guy, but just not for me.

Classic Line(s):

"I'm going to send you this article."

[I received multiple articles as a follow-up to our conversations. I actually liked the interaction.]

"Okay, I am going to take you to Costco. You can use my card and pay cash, but you need to start buying in bulk, girl!"

[As he advises me on the horrific state of our receding economy.]

"If I win the lotto, you won't be able to find me. My number is the first thing I'm disconnecting."

[LOL, good to know! As he proceeded to explain how the first 90 days after winning the lottery are crucial to disappearing to keep people from coming out of the woodwork to ask for money.]

Future Character Attributes:

He had a lot of energy—positive energy—and was a man of the world. Well-read, well-educated, well-informed, and super open-minded. Throw in some quirkiness, and we've got a fun personality to work with here.

Role I Would Assign Him:

I don't know if he would be a leading male in a book (though he could have been in my life if it worked out), but he definitely had that extra cool character vibe that lends wisdom, colorful conversation, and otherwise could bring life to a story outside of the main characters. He'd have to be one of those necessary extras.

My Takeaway:

I don't have the right loan to qualify for federal forgiveness. I need to be a little more mindful of my money. If I want a sugar daddy, then I just have to dress up and go to the Del Mar races. My landlord would benefit from me installing an EV charging station in the garage for the next car I will buy—which will have to be electric, apparently. All joking aside—I love a man who can bring interesting knowledge and conversation to the table, and he certainly did not lack in that department.♥

The Smooth IT Geek

How Far Did He Make It?

Ghosted Right Before First Date

The Backstory:

This guy was my "neighbor." He legitimately was a local guy, so I considered how amazing it would be to date someone close by. Not that we'd always be able to see each other, but I was getting tired of the LA or San Diego connections that would require extensive driving whenever we did meet up. This one seemed to be pretty polished and put together—an intellectual, IT-based professional who had smarts and sex appeal.

Perhaps too much sex appeal, as he'd teeter between casual conversation and YouTube videos about wanting to get into my pants. At the time, I wasn't catching on. And I also wasn't comprehending the gameplay that was going on behind the scenes, as his profile would disappear and reappear a few times due to "glitches."

Anyway, we had finally planned to meet up casually for coffee just to see if there was a "vibe" first. This one was one of my earlier-on deals, where I thought if we kept it simple and liked each other, we could plan a real date and do something fun. Kind of a vetting process for both of us. I'm guessing I read that room incorrectly because when the day came, he had to postpone to an hour later and then another hour, and as he was apologizing, I kept telling him no problem (yes, please keep disrespecting my time and energy).

Well, I guess I finally said something stupid like, it's not a big deal, it's just coffee, and that triggered no further reply or confirmation of our upcoming 5:30p.m. meetup. And so, with no warning, the date never happened, I didn't hear anymore from him, and I let my profile glitch to unmatch. I did find him on another site, with a different version of his name and a different profile style, so I may have dodged a bullet with that one.

Classic Line(s):

"You're so cute and sweet and understanding. A real lady. I can't wait to meet you." **Adds song video: *I Want You* by Snoop Dogg**

[Is it me, or is that mixed messaging?]

"Not sure why you think my profile disappeared. That's weird."

[And yet… he kept disappearing and reappearing.]

"First impressions are everything."

[No impressions are also impressions. Try showing up.]

Future Character Attributes:

I don't know if I got enough out of him to really find something interesting to base any of my characters off of. But I'll shelve it as a possibility—it could be good for some minor traits of one of my characters in an upcoming mystery I'm writing.

Role I Would Assign Him:

He wouldn't warrant a whole role, but I could use some elements of his personality or lifestyle in a supporting character role.

My Takeaway:

Two things: 1) several attempts to reschedule within the same day is a red flag testing to see how far my boundaries can be pushed, and 2) getting sexy music videos is a pretty clear sign of what his intentions are, and coffee is really not of any interest to him.♥

The Too-Nice Shorty

How Far Did He Make It?
Texting

The Backstory:
I'm not going to say anything bad about this guy because I can't. He was super nice and gentlemanly and cool to chat with. We had some shared backgrounds and travel stories, and he was truly interesting to engage with. I don't know why I couldn't give this guy a real chance. This is perhaps where *I* bumbled; he sent me a video of him at a horserace and just didn't look like his pictures, and it was obvious that he was really, really short.

It's shallow, I know. But I'm a bigger girl, and I feel self-conscious with a guy who is both smaller and shorter than me (I can work with one, not both). That being said, he is probably the nicest guy in the world and deserves better than a hypocrite like me. And I really do hope he finds that someone special because he was a sweetheart.

That was a learning experience for me, for sure; I expect someone to overlook my obvious physical flaws, yet I can't look past someone else's? It wasn't a proud moment for me. But I will say, I let him down gently, giving him an excuse of saying work was picking up, and it turned out I didn't have time to date.

A lie, yes—but better than ghosting the poor guy or leading him on. It helps me to sleep at night.

Classic Line(s):

"I don't want to text forever. Would it be okay to get your number?"

[He asked so politely. Told you: gentleman vibes.]

Future Character Attributes:

He just had this really genuine, inquisitive nature about him where he really wanted to know more about me, my travels, and what I loved to do. It didn't even feel like an interview, just a natural asking of questions mixed in with conversation about his own experiences. He was complimentary, open-minded, and super kind. I liked his passion for horseracing and thought that was a cool hobby for a character to have.

Role I Would Assign Him:

The nice guy that a leading lady finally gives a chance to. Wouldn't it be refreshing to read about a guy who didn't have any toxic traits (flaws—but not toxic ones) and was worthy of the caliber of the ingenue?

My Takeaway:

That if I don't want my cover to be judged, I shouldn't judge another's… and that if I was truly looking for love, I needed to give the non-toxic men a fighting chance.♥

The Little Drummer Boy

How Far Did He Make It?
In-app Chats

The Backstory:
He was a really sweet guy, but in all honesty, I think he was just looking for followers on his YouTube channel. It started out with a simple conversation, and we clicked on a few common interests. I thought it was cool that he sent me a video of him playing the drums. I actually like when guys share something real about themselves. It's a great way to see them doing what they love, and you can get a vibe of a person much more off that than endless text convos.

But after the third video and not much in the way of trying to connect by phone or person, I started wondering if he was really looking to date or just wanted exposure. And so, after not having much luck moving forward, I wished him well and called it a day.

Classic Line(s):
"You're kinda far. But you're way too sexy to pass up."
[Didn't realize 30 miles was all that far.]

"I like your style! Hey, check out this video."
[And this video. And this one…]

Future Character Attributes:

I dig guys with musical talent. I did watch a few of his videos, and I liked his drumming—I think it would make for a fun personality trait for some character, male or female, to have. His background in his videos was also pretty cool—material I could use to describe a fun, musically-inspired environment.

Role I Would Assign Him:

I think I could use his eclectic taste in music as part of a friend character I am developing in a soul sister book series, one who is on the artsy side.

My Takeaway:

If they are sending you links to their YouTube, IG, or other promotional handles instead of moving the conversation forward, they might just be looking for followers.♥

CHARACTER PROFILE: THE VAMPIRE LAWYER

What does your character do to show his personality?

(A) First, he shows his intellectual prowess.

(B) Then, he mentally seduces you with his powers of persuasion.

(C) Finally, he grabs you unexpectedly from behind and bites your shoulder.

What does your character look like on the outside?

(A) Iconically tall, dark, and handsome with strong looking hands and broad shoulders.

(B) Full-on professional, clean-cut preppy appearance that's intrinsically deceiving but idyllic.

Name:
District Attorney Igot Fangs

Character Assigned:
Lover with a secret paranormal history of biting his prey as an ancient sex spell.

What does your character say to show his personality?

"I'm looking for someone to stimulate my mind at the table, my soul on the porch, and my body in the bed. Is that too much to ask for?"

What lesson does your character bring about in your story?

You never know what's really lurking beneath the surface. Not everyone that feels like destiny is destiny.

The Vampire Lawyer

How Far Did He Make It?
One Date

The Backstory:

This guy and I matched back and forth over a year and a half period. There was just something about him that kept drawing me back. He was one of the first I connected with online, and he checked off every single box. There was this deep intellectual connection that began where our minds just seemed to be on the same page, talking about books and concepts and pretty much anything in general.

But, at that time, I was insecure and scared, and when he asked to meet, I made an excuse. That led to him being disinterested and ghosting me, and that was a hard lesson for me because I really, really liked him.

Then after I entered and left a relationship, I returned to the online dating scene, and who did I rematch with? The amazing lawyer I couldn't forget. He remembered me physically, but not much else about our conversation (and I, of course, with a disturbing level of memory retention, didn't forget a single fucking thing about him). However, the connection wasn't the same. There was no sharing of books and family history or common interests. It became heavily sexual, and after a while, I became frustrated not being able to reconnect like before, and there was no movement to meet, so I vanished this time.

Months later, we found each other online again. By the third time we matched on a completely different site, I thought

fate was trying to tell me something. Even remembering how frustratingly sextual he was and continued to be (and I indulged him), I knew we HAD to meet. And we finally did.

He surprised me by being the sweetest guy!! I completely expected him to be the typical arrogant and cocky lawyer he projected himself to be over text, yet he was super down to earth, kind, and a complete gentleman. That is, until we got to his apartment to hang out for a little while, and he bit down on me like a vampire and aggressively kissed me. The pain seared through me, and while he didn't break my skin, it was enough to halt things and send me worried to urgent care the next day (I legit had to get a tetanus shot "just in case").

I was lucky; I could have been very hurt that night, and I am super grateful that I had angels looking out for me and protecting me. He was apologetic about being so impulsive and rough, but still... he was not who I had envisioned for over a year and a half since our first match. Needless to say, I fulfilled my aching desire to meet him and moved on without hesitation.

Classic Line(s):

"I'm looking for someone to stimulate my mind at the table, my soul on the porch, and my body in the bed. Is that too much to ask for?"

[No. It's what I want, too... but that's quite the believable line there, buddy. Spoken persuasively like a true lawyer.]

"I don't like to talk on the phone before meeting. It creates expectations that are rarely met."

[But constant texting and sharing doesn't? My expectations were certainly not met.]

"I imagine you wearing a black corset, fishnet stockings, garter, and stilettos. How would you like to be tied up?"

[With silk scarves. Are you buying all that for me?]

Future Character Attributes:

I can't help it, but I love an extremely intelligent man with a bad-boy side. His deep wisdom and knowledge, and even what he shared about cases he had worked on and experiences he had, are grounds for lots of character development. Throw in his sapiosexual-inspired conversations, and I've got some hot sex scenes I can develop… including one if I wanted to turn a normal man into a vampire lover.

Role I Would Assign Him:

Either a straight-up sexy leading man (without the bite gone wrong) or the undercover, otherworldly being hiding behind the mask of a human. Like a lover with a secret paranormal history of biting his prey to cast an ancient sex spell on them. Could be good Sci-Fi material.

My Takeaway:

Not everyone that feels like destiny is destiny. And keep up-to-date on your tetanus shots.♥

The Phone Sex Caretaker

How Far Did He Make It?

Phone Calls

The Backstory:

By this point, you may be questioning some of my morals and common sense. I don't blame you. Keep in mind: these dating profiles are not in order; some happened before the friendly ghost and some after (remember, I have a perverse kind of memory that actually recalls these conversations verbatim, just like the details about my vampire lawyer crush). This date match happened before then, when I was in a bad place and completely broken-hearted, looking for attention.

Here was a man who was also good with his words, intriguing, and interesting as a person. We chatted online for a bit, but he always had a reason for not being able to meet up. He was busy with work; he was ill; he was a caretaker for his parents. In retrospect, he was probably speaking in code for "I'm married," but I indulged his request for a playful phone conversation.

That one call escalated instantly into phone sex, which I had never had at this level before. Sure, I'd play around on the phone with guys I had actually met and dated before but never with some random stranger.

It felt erotic and uninhibited—and left me feeling disturbingly vulnerable afterward, as if we had actual sex and he just up and left without the snuggles. I'm afraid some serious oxytocin was released even without the touch, and that was something

I had never experienced before. It mentally bonded me to this stranger in a way that was uncomfortable.

He continued to dodge requests for a meetup and asked for another phone conversation instead, which was met with my instant unmatch. I was done playing his game.

He did come back around when I returned to the site months later, but it was a pretty quick match/unmatch. He acknowledged we had a connection and that he was in a much different place this time and would like to meet in person. However, he mentioned how hot it would be to meet halfway and just have sex, and I just wasn't feeling like that was something I wanted to do. Just because I allowed it on the phone didn't mean that I wanted to cross that line in person, and I said as much.

Then, after not responding quick enough to another suggestive comment, I guess he got the hint and was gone by the next day. Oh well!

Classic Line(s):

"Answer by saying my name slowly… understood?"

[Oooooo….kkkkkkkkk.]

"I was noting our alignment. We both know good words make us feel more than affinity. They make us hot."

[He kinda had a point there, not gonna lie.]

Future Character Attributes:

He has this mannerism about him that, although very forward sexually, hidden behind this obvious lust, he felt like a hurt or sick little boy who just wanted love and affection. Sexual conversation was his way of expressing his pain or hiding from it. I can see a character development of a man with a traumatic history manifesting in repulsive behavior yet with the potential to be tamed by the right woman or encounter who made him feel safe and vulnerable enough to reveal his true self.

Role I Would Assign Him:

A redeemable leading man who learns how to love and be loved in return. Though, to be honest, I'm tired of reading about these injured men (and experiencing them in real life), so I might not waste time or energy on developing a male character my leading lady has to help heal.

My Takeaway:

That getting so intimate with someone on the phone can release the same confusing endorphins as an in-person connection, leaving you feeling super vulnerable. Be careful.♥

Chef Chatterbox

How Far Did He Make It?

One Date

The Backstory:

This was on and over within two days. We matched, chatted, moved quickly to the phone, hit it off in conversation, and then we both happened to be free that night and made plans to meet up. I was excited—he was a chef with a side business, had roots in the East Coast, and he just had this really intriguing sense of humor and vibe that made me both nervous and hopeful that I was about to meet someone cool.

But I didn't. Who I met was a slob in sweatpants. Now hear me out: he had quite a few hours where he could have stopped quickly back home for even a pair of jeans or shorts. He didn't live that far away; a quick change into something CLEAN would have made a world of difference in caring about his appearance for a first date. Besides that, he was working outside of his house, and thinking he was a professional, I wouldn't have thought the unshowered, grunge, dirty sweats look was acceptable even behind a web meeting camera.

Perhaps that is snobby of me, and I apologize for my professional pretentiousness. (For the record, pajamas would have been more acceptable, believe it or not.)

However, first impressions are everything. I did maturely look past it and give him a chance—only to listen to him drone on and on about how his kids don't like him, how they live in another state, how he can't wait to not have to pay for them or their mother anymore, etc. You kinda don't say that shit to a single mom who has struggled with a man like you and constant child support challenges. Danger, Will Robinson!

Then there were some political and religious turnoffs. Not to mention that he walked us through a café where he worked, grabbed a free cookie (for himself), and didn't even offer to buy me a water. Not a big deal, I can buy my own water—but he didn't even ask me if I wanted to get something for myself, for goodness' sake! We just walked in and out while he enjoyed his cookie.

A half-hour later, I ended up shaking his hand goodbye and then sending a very nice text ending it.

Classic Line(s):

"Sorry I didn't dress up, but I've been here all day."

[Is your washer broken, or was Mommy out of town and unable to do your laundry?]

"I don't really talk to my kids. They don't seem to like me, but maybe when they get older, they will."

[Well, maybe if you put in some effort? IDK, just sayin'.]

Future Character Attributes:

I liked his passion as a chef and, of course, the East Coast attitude. He was funny and witty when he wasn't talking about being a deadbeat dad.

Role I Would Assign Him:

I would not make him into a full character, just parts of his personality would make it into one.

My Takeaway:

Always let a friend be on standby for that all-important call that gives you an out to leave when things go sour… or a pre-determined story about you needing to pick your kid up by a certain time. Thanks, KR, for the escape route on this one!♥

The Italian-Bred Rico Suave

How Far Did He Make It?

Texting

The Backstory:

Ciao, baby. This charmer made his way to me twice. The first time, I was taken in by his Italian sophistication and allure. He was a bit of a romantic, and it was an easy transition from the app to texting on the phone. But that's all that ended up being. We chatted for a bit, but then out of nowhere, the guy just ghosted me. Whatever, I was getting used to that kind of thing by that point, so I simply removed his number and carried on to the next.

But then, a year later, he showed back up, and I figured, what the hell? Curiosity got the better of me, and I swiped back. And he had no clue that we had already not only matched but had extensive text conversations. He claimed he would never forget someone like me, and yet—he did. Whatever. I allowed us to chat for a bit, but then I quickly caught on that he was moving in a more sexual direction, and I just wasn't into playing that game with him. And so, I became the ghost the second time... without feeling bad about it.

Classic Line(s):

"You have the most beautiful smile. It must be beautiful to wake up to."

[Thank you. Very charming, but not going to work.]

"I would never forget a woman as beautiful as you."

[Um, clearly, you would because you did.]

Future Character Attributes:

Some more European influence to work with. I liked some of the lines he used, so they could show up somewhere, but I'm not sure he really is an inspiration for a full character.

Role I Would Assign Him:

None really. Just use of his foreign attributes and one-liners.

My Takeaway:

Just because they come back around for a second shot, it doesn't mean I have to swipe right as if they will be different this time. If they already showed you who they were the first time, believe them.♥

SETTING THE SCENE
ROMANTIC HISTORIC CABIN

What imagery has been inspired?

(A) Rustic lake cabin restored back to Prohibition times.

(B) Winter: snow on the ground, old school fireplace, blankets and hot cocoa or a glass of wine on the couch.

What moment has been inspired?

(A) Being snowed in and forced to finally face that the adversarial feelings are simply denied attraction.

(B) Hot and steamy sex scene to melt the ice.

Artwork Credit: Iryna Krylova)Depositphotos.com

The Gaslighting Wine Mayor

How Far Did He Make It?

Video Calls/Endless Texting

The Backstory:

This was an interesting one. Lots of back and forth. He was smart, a mayor with a second home in a lake community, and intriguing with random trivia-like knowledge. We hit it off immediately and went quickly to phone texts and then to a FaceTime tour of his absolutely gorgeous cabin. Talk about a romantic setting!

He wanted to teach me all about wine and how to pair it with different meals and saw it as a fun challenge to illuminate me. I was game, but I had to work out a few scheduling things on my end before I could make the trip a bit up north to where his cabin was.

Things were going well but went sideways quickly. My son was selling candy bars for a fundraiser, and he had a friend who coincidentally lived in my town go there to buy candy. I didn't get to meet his friend, however, because my son banished me from standing with him. I was a bit relieved because I was a little freaked out about this guy sending a friend just to scope me out.

I don't know why I let it bother me, but it did. But what was worse is that after he told me his friend had stopped by, I didn't hear from him the rest of the night—not until noon the next day. I admit I did get into my head and let it worry me a little that his friend reported back something negative, and here I was, ghosted. But I stopped the brain chatter and decided to give him the benefit of the doubt that he just got drunk, and I'd hear from him when he recovered.

So the next day, I turned my phone off, and me and the kids drove down south to an orchard for the day. It was an amazing day with them—some much-needed quality time. Well, around 3 p.m., I turn my phone back on to see multiple messages waiting for me.

First, the apology for not getting back to me; he got hammered. But then, after I hadn't responded within 90 minutes, I got the "are you ignoring me?" and then "I guess you are, have a nice life" texts.

Seriously... This guy took 18 hours to respond after we left off mid-conversation the night prior, and I take only a few hours to respond because I am with my kids and literally driving two hours back to my house. He said he thought I was ghosting him, but I didn't want to deal with his insecurities on top of my own, and I just shut down for the rest of the day. Not gonna lie... the way he was handling a few different situations up to and including this point felt like gaslighting.

The next day, I reached out to talk through it and was told I overthink and was too far for anything real, so he was going to keep me at arm's length. Okay, fine. We chatted back and forth a little (yes, I realized I should have shut it down by then, but he had a really nice cabin. I wanted to see it). Eventually, it got to the point where I had enough and told him I wished him the best. Then he came roaring back with the interest of wanting to at least stay text friends. I agreed but didn't text any further, and then within two days, he was back to being the initiating communicator.

That didn't last long. There were a few more mishaps along the way, including an issue with an unsolicited pic out of nowhere, which I set his ass straight about, and a bunch of going back and forth for yet another few days with no solidified plans to meet up. Finally, I gave up.

His cabin was no longer worth my time and effort, as much as I wanted to see it more than I wanted to see him. Not sorry. It looked like it could have made for a very romantic setting, and I was willing to make the trip for the ambiance alone. Oh well! Next!

Classic Line(s):

"I'm only 5'8, so if you want taller, I can wear heels."

[Cute and funny. I liked it. I told him I'm 5'6", and that worked for me because that meant I could wear flats and not fall on my face.]

"Sounds like you're the perfect woman. When do we start?"

[Is this a job interview? Did you just hire me? I'm confused.]

"Did you stop talking to me? … Oh, guess so. I'll stop texting. Have a nice life."

[Is this where we play the 'I should have my phone on at all times game while you take full days to respond' game? No thanks!]

Future Character Attributes:

I really liked his prominence in his community and his wine connoisseur education. I found it cultural and cute. I also absolutely adored the FaceTime tour of his cabin, which he had restored back to Prohibition times, and if that isn't a setting for a romantic novel, I don't know what is.

Role I Would Assign Him:

A really sophisticated leading man—time period character, most likely. Even though I didn't get to see it in person, I definitely will be using the cabin scenery—I have pics and a good memory from my virtual tour to make it work!

My Takeaway:

Sometimes it's okay to stick it out for the experience of something new... but don't hold out too long for it. Otherwise it just becomes a game, and that's not worth wasting either of your time. ♥

The Never-Ending Pen Pal

How Far Did He Make It?

In-app Chats

The Backstory:

This guy was one of my earlier-on matches when I didn't know how this all really worked and that endless texting within the app was really a bad sign that it was going nowhere fast. I swear, I think we texted daily for like three or four weeks before I finally said enough. And I didn't suggest exchanging numbers or meeting up because even though on this particular site I met him, it's ladies who reach out first, I still wanted to give the man the opportunity to make the next move. I wanted him to ask me for my number or for a date.

Call me old-fashioned, but I was trying to be both progressive and traditional as I navigated this really weird way of dating people. I soon learned after that that if it stays too long in text mode, it's not moving forward.

There's a balance between a slow burn, a 'getting to know you' vibe, and a cool pen pal. But at least this guy wasn't a sexter; he was just a writer who loved to write back and forth with me.

Classic Line(s):

"What kind of dinner will you have waiting for your hunk when he gets home?"

[Take out. And if you're truly a hunk? Then we're not eating dinner.]

Future Character Attributes:

I liked his sweet, relaxed nature. His chill writer vibe. His cool way of expressing himself and what interested him. He was a soothing person to talk to, with very little drama, which is probably why I allowed it for so long.

Role I Would Assign Him:

A side character who was an introverted writer—or even a narrator! Oh, that could be a cool character. He could be the writer of the novel I am writing. I kinda dig that impromptu insight I just got sitting here reflecting on him. Hmm.

My Takeaway:

If a conversation doesn't progress beyond in-app texting to at least an in-app video chat or call within a week or two, it's a pretty clear sign that it ain't going anywhere. Move on. ♥

The Sex-Obsessed Security Guard

How Far Did He Make It?
Video Chat/Canceled First Date

The Backstory:

The guy with two names (given and preferred) was actually a real contender until our conversations went sideways and I uncovered another potential narcissist. But before I did, we quickly had a connection that was full of humor, intellect, openness, and even vulnerability. He was super easy to talk to, even with uncomfortable conversations.

There was a balance in the communication at first between getting to know each other on a friend level and sexual curiosity, with him understanding my boundaries for when we met. And he said he respected them completely. So, I proceeded cautiously.

Well, we were supposed to meet up one day, but then I got the call that he was exhausted from work that morning: could we reschedule? I was hesitant to believe that based on past cancellation experiences. I mean, I know for myself that when I get tired, I don't really feel like going out, but I push myself because I want to see that person, and I always am glad I made the choice to go instead of canceling. I thought that if he wanted to meet me, he'd make that effort, especially since I was willing to drive toward him. But no, it remained canceled.

He did end up FaceTiming me, and I don't know if it was because I was disappointed or something else, but I instantly felt a lack of interest in seeing him after that. I pushed through that thought, but not for long. The next day, I couldn't talk because it was Easter, and then I had a work deadline to meet—and he began to turn it around on me that I was too busy for him. Yet, I was still in communication with him and called him every morning from my walks and every evening to talk about our day. And he continued to drive conversations toward sex after I had explicitly asked him to back off—to which he seemingly agreed—and then accused me of encouraging his suggestive innuendos, so what did I expect?

A few more subtle gaslighting comments as the week went on, and I caught onto the narcissism game. Nope. Not this time. I shut it down and just told him I didn't think it was going to work out between us. I told him straight up that he was making me uncomfortable with how much he talked about sex and rarely anything else anymore, and that's not what I was looking for.

Only a few months later, he pops back up in my match pile. I swiped back only because I was curious to see what he wanted. Was it an apology? An attempt to try to actually meet me? Why would this guy want to match with me again after the way we left things?

Well, I'm all about closure, so if he needed to say something, I'd let him, then close the door again. But when I asked him why he swiped right, he just said he was confused and didn't understand that I only matched him because I saw he had swiped first—it was clear that this was going to be another gaslighting game. So I bounced, and that was the end of that one.

But, in our more interesting conversations, I learned about a little town north of me called Solvang that he loved to ride his bike to, and that single travel tip ended up being an important road trip later on for me. So, the craziness was worth being led to something even cooler.

Classic Line(s):

"I don't mean any disrespect, but I want to fuck the shit out of you."

[Thanks?]

"You are so different from all of the other girls I've met. I can't wait to see you later."

[Later: cancels date because he's too tired.]

"Oh, okay. Your 'friend.' Whatever."

[His response to me telling him that my girlfriend and her son, who are like family to us, were still over at my house on EASTER and I couldn't talk, and he didn't believe me.]

"I'm confused. I matched you?"

[He was in my 'inbox,' so I matched to ask him if there was something he wanted to say. More games. Nope.]

Future Character Attributes:

I liked his combination of being a tough guy and a teddy bear. Funny and serious. Both down to earth and adventurous. He had some redeeming personality qualities that I would definitely want to work into different characters. Just not the game-playing ones. I could use his gaslighting lines and tactics in another abuse novel, though.

Role I Would Assign Him:

I'm not sure I would use him as a single character unless it was someone who travels to amazing places on his motorcycle.

My Takeaway:

Dear Jenny, remember to acknowledge the red flags instead of just watching them wave.♥

The Straight Shooter

How Far Did He Make It?

Multiple Phone Calls

The Backstory:

I liked this guy's brutal honesty. I could tell that he was a pretty straight shooter from the get-go—not afraid to speak his mind. But it was never in a disrespectful or abusive way. His delivery was always forward but sensitive, if that makes any sense. We had a few great phone conversations, and then he asked me if I wanted to meet up.

But I wasn't sure by that point if I was feeling the connection, as cool as he seemed. Or I was afraid. I might have been feeling a little insecure after adding on a few unwanted pounds and was worried about the whole "fatfishing" thing I had just learned about. My pictures were truthful and unfiltered, and yet, did they really see me? Or did they just look at my main profile with just my face?

I didn't want to travel up to LA just to be rejected. I was tired that week and wanted to bail. So, I made excuses, like I was super busy with work. I thought if I could buy myself two weeks to get those water-weight pounds off, I'd feel better and could go through with it. (Hey, just being real here. I never said I was the perfect catch without flaws and insecurities.)

He called me out on my shit. He told me that even when we are busy, we can make time for the things that are important in life. He was right. It was something I told myself whenever I heard the words "I'm too busy" from my own potential dates. And while I ultimately chose not to pursue him, I did appreciate his candor, and he was right: I was full of shit, and I had to stop and take a long, hard look at my readiness to date at that time.

If I wasn't prepared to show up, I had no business making new connections.

Classic Line(s):

"You'd make the time if you really wanted to, punkin."
[Dang. He was absolutely right.]

"Are you too independent for a man?"
[No, but I don't think I have to give up my independence in order to deeply share my life with someone.]

Future Character Attributes:

Clearly, his refreshing honesty. He was candid yet cool. He knew how to get his point across without being condescending, even if the truth was something I didn't want to hear. And I like that for a strong male character somewhere.

Role I Would Assign Him:

I can see him either as a straightforward leading male or that amazing best friend that helps you to get out of your own way by unapologetically telling you the truth.

My Takeaway:

That if I'm not into someone, just end it and move on. Making excuses is immature and unfair. ♥

CHARACTER PROFILE:
THE FRUGAL VALI-DATER

What does your character do to show his personality?

(A) Not a frequent communicator, but consistent when he does communicate.

(B) Rushes us to the parking lot to validate our tickets.

(C) Demonstrates sweetness, but an inability to flirt on the most basic of levels.

What does your character look like on the outside?

(A) Tall, broad, bigger guy, but more on the stocky side.

(B) Didn't really get too dressed up for dates, but not a slob either - we'll just give him a li'l bit of a fashion overhaul.

Name:
Mr. McSavings

What does your character say to show his personality?

"OK, so if we parked at 4:57, then we have 13 minutes for validation. We should get moving."

Character Assigned:
Your everyday boy-next-door type of guy that you "should" end up with.

What lesson does your character bring about in your story?

Quirks can be cute and are not necessarily dealbreakers. Give an eccentric guy a chance and see how much you can learn from him.

The Frugal Vali-dater

❦

How Far Did He Make It?

Two Dates

The Backstory:

He was a sweet guy. Very soothing energy, and I immediately felt comfortable in his presence. He felt very familiar to me—not that fated feeling like we knew each other in a past life and have come together again type thing (yes, I've had that before) but a very relaxed knowing just the same. It made for very easy conversation without any nerves whatsoever.

We chatted a few times on the phone, and he was both easy to talk to and man enough to make plans and stick with them. It was nice not to have to do the work.

He had mentioned a really cool place in Disney I hadn't heard of and was going to look into taking me there. Super cool, right?

Well, of course, the planner that I am tried to sneak a peek at availability to find that there was none—you needed to reserve 60 days in advance. But when he texted me that it was a no-go for there, he said it was because they were the only place that didn't validate parking.

Okay, I thought. Interesting that he checked that out before seeing that there wasn't even availability, but I could understand that being an important factor, as Disney can be expensive. I was content with him finding an alternate happy hour place for us to go to in a cool area.

We met, and there was this huge convention filling up the bar. The table service was completely empty, but he grabbed my hand and pulled me into the crowd, saying we were going to the bar (Side note: I would have still ordered off the happy hour menu and offered to pay my portion if we sat in the regular section).

He saw a table where we could sit that wasn't cleaned off yet, and the check was still on it, but we sat anyway. I tried to curb my OCD and not freak out that we were seated at a dirty high-top surrounded by tons of conference goers—drunk and friendly.

Once I got past that, I thought the date went really well. Conversation and laughs were flowing, we chatted with some of the surrounding people, and I thought he was a really nice guy that I wouldn't mind spending more time with. We decide to leave the restaurant and walk around the area—until he approached the hostess stand to validate our parking and found out we had only thirteen minutes until times up.

I told him we still had a few minutes to walk around, but he was this nervous nelly as we did, so I just guided us back toward the pay machine to make him better. I told him I wouldn't have cared, that it was only $3 to park, but he insisted that we needed to get these validated before time was up. I took it to mean the date was over!

And it was. He walked me to my car, hugged me twice, and then asked me if I'd like to get together again to do "fun things." Now, he didn't kiss me, and he wasn't very flirty, so I am pretty sure his "fun things" meant discounted tickets to a local show where there is free parking and no sex, so I agreed. Why not? Not everything has to move fast, and aside from his validation paranoia and coupon-cutting shares (I learned a lot about deals), I did feel comfortable with him, and he was a kind, decent man.

Right after our date, he went on a little trip and sent me photos of everything he was doing—not to brag or anything, but because he wanted to share his experience with me. I liked that he did that and was coming to realize that he was quirky but sweet, and I was looking forward to seeing him again in person.

We made plans to see an immersive art exhibit, and not only was he a fellow experience junkie, but he also loved a good deal! (Coupon for 'buy one ticket, get one free' was a jackpot!) The experience was an absolute bust, and we found ourselves uncertain about what to do next. I gave him an out to leave if he wanted, but he pulled me in for a hug and gave me these puppy dog eyes and told me he wanted to stay and spend time with me. It was the first time I felt any real interest from him, and it was cute.

We ended up going to the Griffith Observatory after being able to park handicapped for free (he drove all over LA that day for us since he could park everywhere for free. I can't make this up). We seemed to enjoy our time there together, and he even stole a sweet kiss from me in the elevator and wrapped his arms around me as we overlooked the Hollywood sign. I thought he was warming up, and I could see the potential. We left saying we wanted to see each other again, with him saying he'd come to me this time and parted with a brief kiss and teddy bear hug.

But it just wasn't enough of a fire to keep burning for me. Ultimately, the texts dwindled down. He'd didn't try to make another plan, we never got to a third date, and his flirting skills were pretty underwhelming. Great guy, but I need someone with a little more oomph, passion, and effort.

He was so kind as we ended things, and I wish it could have worked out differently, but I do need a man who shows interest in seeing me or even having a conversation more than once a month. Sometimes casual is too casual, and I was looking to build something stronger.

Classic Line(s):

"You have such a friendly, welcoming smile. Great energy."
[Aww. Sweet.]

"I'm looking forward to our visit tonight."
[Visit? Is my aunt coming to town? I thought this was a date?]

"OK, so if we parked at 4:57, then we have 13 minutes for validation. We should get moving."
[Um, ok, guess that's my signal this date is over.]

"I am very thankful for the time that we got to spend together. You have wonderful energy and a brilliant personality. Thank you for what we shared."
[Sniff. The sweetest goodbye I had ever heard. It made me sad that I made the move to end things.]

Future Character Attributes:

This is hard to say. He was very open and honest, caring, non-judgmental, and sweet. Kind of like your everyday boy-next-door type of guy. His frugal obsession was amusing, but I'm not sure it was character-worthy.

Role I Would Assign Him:

It would probably be a nice friend. That someone you can count on that remains more platonic but supportive rather than a romantic lead. Or better yet—the good guy you really should end up with (who shows interest, of course).

My Takeaway:

Go on dates where there is free parking, otherwise your date will last only as long as the validation time period. Kidding. Quirks can be cute and are not necessarily dealbreakers. Give an eccentric guy a chance and see how much you can learn from him. ♥

The Mansplainer

How Far Did He Make It?

Phone Videos/Ghosted First Date

The Backstory:

I am drawn to men with New York roots, and this guy was from Brooklyn. They have this edge that can't be found in California natives, and I dig it. He was no different, except his profile said he wanted to go beyond the normal conversations and dive deep into dreams and soulful conversations. Perfect. I was in.

For over a month, we'd text, and then he started doing something super cute: sending me videos. Since we were both busy, and since he hated texting, he'd record a good morning or general hello or good night—all completely appropriate and sweet. I liked it so much that I sent him videos back, and it was a way for us to talk when we couldn't chat on the phone yet still see each other. He also had this incredible smile. He was a bigger man than I might have normally gone out with, but considering my own flaws, I wasn't going to judge or not explore the potential opportunity. Did I mention his smile???

Well, I was going out with girlfriends one night in his area and told him where I'd be if he wanted to drop by. I kept him posted on my ETA but then didn't hear from him, so I stopped updating him. He didn't show up, which was totally fine, but the next day, he asked me what had happened. He thought I was going to text when I actually got there, and I was waiting to hear from him to see if he was even interested in meeting up. So it was a simple matter of miscommunication. So then we had made plans for just us to meet up the next weekend.

Things were going along like normal, and I had asked him what he wanted to do that Sunday. He didn't respond, so I figured he was just busy with work. Then I saw he unmatched me, which was weird. But then what was weirder was two hours later, he texted me good night. So I played along and asked again about Sunday. No response. So then the next morning, I told him I noticed he unmatched and that I guess I had my answer, but that it was nice chatting with him anyway. He immediately responds that he was deleting his account, that he was still very interested, and that things have just been crazy at work.

I replied with a simple okay, but I guess that was misconstrued as a kiss-off because he didn't reach out again to make plans. And that was the end of it—until he sent me a random video that mansplained why guys stop texting (because they want to see if women are interested enough. Yeah, that falls under the game-playing category, and I'm out).

Classic Line(s):

"You are exquisite. Your smile is radiant."
[Talk to me like that allll dayyy longggg.]

"What? You don't like men with some meat on them?"
[I don't shy away from dad bods. We both have extra cuddle potential, LOL.]

"I woke up this morning and watched your video. Such a nice way to wake up in the morning to roll over and see your face."
[I'm not going to touch that…]

"OMG, my heart just skipped a beat. You're so adorable. Just wanna bite you."
[After my vampire experience, that made me a little nervous.]

Future Character Attributes:

I liked his innovation with the videos. I can see that becoming a cool, modern kind of communication in a love story when they are having a long-distance relationship instead of just FaceTime. I think it was pretty fun to exchange back-and-forth clips (with the exception of the ghost mansplaining video).

Role I Would Assign Him:

I'm not sure he'd make it into a role. Though some of his one-liners will make it to the narrative, I can tell you that!

My Takeaway:

Videos are a great way to get to know someone or say hello when your schedules are crazy and you can't connect at the same time. It gives it a more personal touch than just a text. ♥

Clark Kent Look-Alike

How Far Did He Make It?

Phone Call/Canceled date

The Backstory:

This guy legitimately looked like Superman's alter ego—a sexy look with male librarian glasses and everything. I was in a rebound mode after a major rejection and had put a temporary pause on my morals to consider this very-forward, obvious one-night-stand guy—well, if after at least a coffee, I found him as attractive and appealing as I did online.

It almost became another phone sex arrangement, leading to a 'let's meet and hookup' situation, but I kept hesitating on fully committing to either—because, in fact, I didn't *want* to pause my morals and jump into bed with some random stranger to get over someone else. I was just hurting and thought that was what I needed and wanted at the time.

I'll share an added twist of my weirdness during this time of dilemma if you promise not to judge me too harshly. (Oh, fuck it. Judge me. I'm totally okay with it.) I was curious as to how all astrological signs were in bed and figured out which signs I had been with and which were left to "try." (I know… Pain can make you bizarre sometimes). As a Cancer, he was on my list of 1 signs I hadn't slept with yet, so I thought he'd check off a bucket list item in the process.

Well, thanks to him playing games on the day we were supposed to meet up, I alternatively found my cojones and declared I wasn't an option. I told him as much and then blocked and moved on. I was quite proud of myself for thinking straight and making a better choice. I have since worked through it with my therapist and discarded my ridiculous Astro-sex bucket list and am now functioning once again as a sane female trying to find the diamonds in the rough, regardless of their sun sign (except Gemini. I have to RUN from Geminis, like, forever).

I'm also not judging myself or anyone else who finds themselves in this situation; I just know, deep in my heart, that this kind of planned meaningless interaction would have left me more empty than fulfilled, so I was ultimately happy with the ways things turned out.

Classic Line(s):

"GM, I'm horny."

[Congratulations.]

"I'm free all weekend. I'm yours... Tell me the day and time." *{We set a date for an undetermined time in the morning. That morning:}* "I was out of town this morning, remember?"

[Nope. Never said that. Planning then canceling a date as if I was an option in his calendar? Hard pass.]

"So you're breaking up with me?"

[After I told him I was no one's option and that I wasn't interested in pursuing this.]

Future Character Attributes:

I know that Clark Kent has already been "done," but I can't help but want to use the "look wholesome but internally naughty" kind of appeal he had.

Role I Would Assign Him:

I couldn't make him a leading man. He'd have to be a deceiving supporting character where he appeared one way but, in reality, was another because of having an alter-ego. It depends on how it goes as I write it and release it, but I may use this decoy idea in a mystery I'm writing at the same time as I'm writing this. I guess we'll see!

My Takeaway:

Continue to recognize when I'm being considered an option and act accordingly. And set a hard no on the phone sex, meetup sex, and other premature sex offerings because they just aren't for me.♥

The Real Estate Workaholic

---❧♥❧---

How Far Did He Make It?

One date

The Backstory:

I really, really liked this guy. We had chemistry on multiple levels: intellectual, professional, sense of humor, physical, spiritual, common interests—you name it, we matched up pretty well. Our phone conversations were respectful, fun, and enlightening. We had so much in common and were both excited about our first date. But there was a little bump on the way there.

I was going to drive down to him for dinner, but I hadn't heard from him yet that he was done with work and ready to meet up. Real estate wasn't always predictable. And neither were dates, as I had come to know by this point. But that didn't matter—I was heading down there anyway.

I decided that if he was about to cancel, I looked too cute and had the night off, so I was going to take myself to dinner on the water. So, by the time he called to check in, I was already en route somewhere along the way.

I feel like he had the intention to reschedule, and I told him he could if he wanted and that I had no problem going out to dinner by myself and enjoying a beautiful Friday evening with or without him. Well, he quickly reconsidered and offered a place for us to meet up and have that date. I agreed cautiously, feeling like I already saw the signs that this wouldn't fare well. And when I met him, I was underwhelmed—until we started talking.

We hit it off big time. We talked and laughed and flirted, and he was the touchy type, though not in a disrespectful way. At no point during our getting-to-know-you talks did we mention sex, so it was nice to experience a date without having that stupid expectation over my head.

But then he kept trying to kiss me in the restaurant, which made me feel uncomfortable. I'm a romantic, but I like at least the first kiss to be private before we venture out to PDA. And I kept trying to communicate that, and then when we walked outside along the water, he understood I wasn't trying to reject him once we finally did kiss.

That kiss was off the charts, which I didn't expect at all. He was a much better kisser than I anticipated. Like a really good kisser. Of course, he offered for us to continue the date at his place, but I declined. He seemed to respect that, we kissed some more, and I begrudgingly let him walk me back to my car. I didn't really want the night to end, but I owed it to myself to respect my own boundaries.

I thought we'd be going on a second date after that. He called immediately after we parted and asked me when he could see me again. I told him tentatively in a week because I had a huge work project that I needed to handle, and he said that it was okay and that he couldn't wait to see me again. We texted a little after that—nothing too eager or overwhelming; it felt natural. It wasn't even every day, but still enough to feel connected.

But then I had an opening during the week and asked if he was available to meet up. He said yes, it would work... and then, that day, he canceled and said he was too busy with work that night, but we were still on for Sunday. I was fine with it; I'm a professional, and work happens, and I had no reason to believe that I was being blown off.

But then, he was too busy for Sunday... and in general. Out of nowhere. No more texts, calls, and no plans for another date. It didn't add up at all. I couldn't figure out for the life of me what had gone wrong. I thought maybe he changed his mind because I didn't go back to his place (too bad), but the weird thing about that is that he actually told me that the last girl he dated he hung out with five times at his house and never even kissed her—and that he was surprised himself that he was kissing me at that moment.

It ended up being a very confusing ghosting situation, but c'est la vie. Guess I won't always get an answer as to why someone just didn't want to pursue something.

Classic Line(s):

"Are you trying to make me fall for you?"

[As he comes in for an unexpected kiss. If I was trying, guess I failed?]

"I have a thing for blondes with cute feet."

[In person, it sounds a lot less creepy than if that were texted to me.]

Future Character Attributes:

His sense of humor. His love of the arts and music. His extroverted, sociable personality. His affectionate nature. His manners. His unapologetic manliness to just kiss me because he wanted to without being afraid. He really was powerfully masculine in a very appealing way.

Role I Would Assign Him:

Aside from his disappearing on me, he otherwise was a truly interesting, strong man that could serve as a good lead male character. I'll just leave out the part of him that flakes out without warning.

My Takeaway:

Sometimes I am never going to understand why it didn't work out, and just have to accept it instead of overanalyzing "what I did wrong." I didn't do anything wrong; I guess it just wasn't right for him, and by extension, he wasn't right for me. ♥

Actual poem he wrote to me, which I did tweak and incorporate into another book, but here I left it unedited to preserve its authenticity:

There was a blue eye girl, I scarcely knew, she had a smile that lit up the room, we spoke through our awkwardness, and laughed at the incredible, that will most differently manifest, it's inevitable.

We merged into one, but she was stunned as I blew up her phone to reach her, as I was her teacher, as her tone was but a moan, of all she would not let in, was me in the end.

As I let out a groan and sigh, I smiled and kissed her gently on her forehead between her eyes.

I held her for a moment, and released her like a dove, forever knowing her my love.

The Spiritual Narcissist

How Far Did He Make It?

Multiple Phone Calls/Canceled First Date

The Backstory:

This complex man was my very first online connection. We met on a spiritually-based dating website where I thought I would find a quality man in alignment with my spiritual path who would understand some of my metaphysically-smitten quirkiness.

It began as a whirlwind; one conversation had us believing in fate. There were so many astrological, numerical, and experiential connections that it was too good to be true. He seemed enamored with me, not caring about my physical flaws, and truly interested in everything about me. I had never experienced that before; I was always the pursuer or the one more interested.

We'd talk for hours until I had to force myself off the phone to sleep a little. We'd text all day long. It was so amazing to feel so wanted by someone for what seemed to be all the right reasons. He actually liked *me* as a person.

And then it became too much. Too much texting. Too many music videos. Too many declarations of forever. Too many red flags I was sensing but ignoring. My requests for him to back off a little bit and not blow up my phone or give me a night off from calling so I could get sleep were met with resistance. And yet, I still wanted to meet this man. On paper, he offered so much that I looked for in a man that I had never received from any other man before. So much so that I ignored all warnings.

Dear Bumbling Boy...

Finally, we were set to go on a date. I bought a new dress, and it was the happiest I'd been in a long time. It was going to be my first real date since I moved to California five years earlier, actually. I was over the moon, and everything was in place—I easily had a sitter for my kids, and it all just lined up perfectly. Until I got the call that he had a weird rash on his face, and he didn't know what to do.

I told him I didn't care if he had a nervous rash and that I still wanted to meet him. I told him to give it an hour, and if what I suggested didn't help him, then we could reschedule. Two hours later, I hadn't heard back from him at all. And so, being pissed and hurt, I went for a walk and instead decided to call a girlfriend and meet up for a drink. I wasn't going to wait around all night for the inevitable cancellation.

He called a few hours later, way past our meetup time, and I pretty much blew him off. The next night, he finally came around, but I was out with another girlfriend (pre-planned) for her birthday. I didn't pick up, and he left a nasty message, basically berating me for not being there for him—he ended up in the ER, scared about his face, but I found it more important to go to a party with my friends than to be by his side.

That was the moment I woke up and saw him for who he was: a full-blown, love-bombing narcissist. He had successfully pulled me into his web, and I almost repeated history. Luckily, I got out before I even got in. I ended up saying what I needed to say and then blocked... but not before he sent a final condescending poem to me that made me roll my eyes with both relief and laughter that I dodged a huge bullet.

And the dress I bought for our date? I wore it instead a week later to a wedding—the one in which I married myself and vowed to always honor myself above all others. It was poetically perfect.

Classic Line(s):

"You know who you are talking to, right? Your future husband. Get me your ring size."

[Like an idiot, I thought we had a fated connection and bought into it, LOL.]

"You really let me down. I can't believe you chose to go out with your friends instead of being there for me. You have no idea how you really hurt me."

[After he canceled our date because he went to the "ER" because of this skin rash, and then, somehow, without knowing his last name or address, expected me to know where he was.]

"I sent 222 messages. Found this rabbit on the side of the road. This bride doll. Our birthdays and the 4:44. These are all signs, and you are just going to walk away from the best thing that will ever happen to you in your life?"

[Yes. Yes, I fucking am.]

Future Character Attributes:

If I were to write another book about a narcissistic man, I would have plenty of material to work off of in terms of the love-bombing and gaslighting I experienced with this guy. In fact, I did work some of his actual words and actions into the main male character of my *Beat Me With Your Words* novel already.

Role I Would Assign Him:

Although already used for one of my characters, there were plenty of conversations from which to build additional characters in future abuse novels I have planned. 222 text messages worth.

My Takeaway:

Believe the red flags when you see them, and don't buy into the love-bombing and gaslighting. Run like fucking hell. ♥

The Food-Obsessed Investor

─────────────❦─────────────

How Far Did He Make It?

Multiple Phone Calls

The Backstory:

What intrigued me about this guy was his blunt honesty—and I appreciated it. Raise your hand if you have any clue how to really break the ice and ask questions to sound interesting enough to capture their attention. I didn't, and apparently, I came off as a reporter; he almost unmatched because he felt like I was conducting an interview instead of trying to converse naturally. So, that helped me to see that my approach was a little too methodical, and he kindly gave me a chance to redeem myself.

Which ended up with him asking me questions, interview-style. Go figure.

Anyway, we progressed to having a few phone calls, but ultimately, he bored me to tears. All he could talk about was food—what he ate, where he was going to eat, how it was Taco Tuesday again—and unusual music events. Now, I love music, but these were obscure events, and I just wasn't feeling the vibe. He was into investments, and his humor was literally of a Beavis and Butthead nature. As in, he quoted them.

I mean, he was a really nice guy, and I could have given him a chance to meet up at least, but instead, we mutually ghosted, and that was the end of that.

Classic Line(s):

"You are obviously in interview mode, and I don't do interviews."

[Was glad he pointed that out, and I adjusted my approach… then he started asking me questions like he was the interviewer. Hmm.]

Future Character Attributes:

I liked his honesty and directness and his delivery of it. But not sure there was much else to pull from.

Role I Would Assign Him:

Poor guy. Not sure he's going to make it into a character of mine. Or maybe that's lucky for him?

My Takeaway:

My approach was too professional and not warm and engaging enough. That was a good experience for me, and I was glad he was honest enough to address it so I could learn from it.

The Wandering Landlord

———————————❦———————————

How Far Did He Make It?
Phone Calls

The Backstory:

He was a super nice guy, but whenever we talked, he always sounded very confused—most likely, he was just high. He didn't do much for work because he owned and rented out a lot of homes, so he just took care of things as he needed to for his tenants and spent his free time where else? Surfing.

He'd mention coming to my area and wanting to get together but never followed up that he was actually coming or here. And then would call the next day to say he was coming up again, maybe in two days, but again, after trying to figure out the code for how to actually make a tentative plan with him, there would be confused crickets.

It was weird and erratic, and he wasn't your typical game player, even though on paper, it sounds like it. I think he just legitimately had no fucking clue what he was doing or where he was going and was high 24/7. I did let him know that I thought he was sweet but that it wasn't going to work, and he was so kind in his response. I'm sure he is a lovely person, but I need a little more stability in a man.

Classic Line(s):

"So chill to meet another INTJ. Right on."

[Not sure that means automatic compatibility anymore after speaking with him.]

Future Character Attributes:

His job was cool, I guess. I didn't have much else to work with, even from the few conversations we had.

Role I Would Assign Him:

I think this might be another one who didn't really impact me enough. Sorry, guy.

My Takeaway:

When you kindly disconnect the connection, you can feel the appreciation for acting like a human instead of a bitch. It never hurts to be mature and let someone down gently instead of simply disappearing.♥

The Dutch Widower

How Far Did He Make It?
Multiple Phone Calls

The Backstory:
He was a truly kind, in-it-for-the-right-reasons type of guy. He was Dutch and brought some traditional, honest family values with him to the table. His wife had died a few years prior from cancer, and he was looking for someone to share his life with. He didn't have kids, and he didn't once talk about getting together for sex. All positive flags thus far in my book, so we exchanged numbers and talked for a little bit. And being a sucker for an accent, it only heightened his adorability.

However, he became overbearing too fast and expected too much too soon from someone he had yet to meet in person. I had to explain what I was doing every night (I read. I legit read obsessively. Or I otherwise am watching television with my kids). He didn't like how long it took me to finish what I was doing before calling or texting goodnight.

I don't like men who are clingy or needy; I need a decent amount of space, at least as I am getting to know someone. So, I ended it and wished him luck.

Classic Line(s):
"Are you done reading? I'm waiting for you to say good night."
[Um, I did already say good night, letting you know that I would be lost in a book. No one puts a time limit on Baby's reading.]

Future Character Attributes:

Again, it's the European thing that gets me, but instead of the suave type, he was the wholesome, good human type. I could use that as a foundation for an amazing male character—just without the clingy co-dependency.

Role I Would Assign Him:

I can't really put my finger on it yet, but he could definitely inspire an overseas character that the main characters interact with or who even was the main love interest.

My Takeaway:

If I'm not enjoying good night texts or calls or avoiding them in favor of a book, I'm not really interested. ♥

CHARACTER PROFILE: SENSUAL SHAKESPEARE

Name: Romeo

What does your character do to show his personality?

A. Uses words to poetically capitivate my interest.

B. Shares his own experiences and challenges with writing.

C. Attempts to mansplain intimacy vs. passion.

What's in a name? That which we call a rose by any other name would smell as sweet.

What does your character look like on the outside?

A. Another bearded guy...what's up with this trend? Let's make it just sexy scruff.

B. From the photos, he had kind, sensitive eyes and a sweet, pouty mouth (in a manly way).

What does your character say to show his personality?

"I'd happily barter my cooking skills with your clean-up skills if you'd consider sweetening the pot with some kisses & cuddling."

Character Assigned:
Outwardly tough leading man who has a softer side from being a secret writer.

What lesson does your character bring about in your story?

Clearly communicate your boundaries. Let down your guard for vulnerability, but not for manipulation.

Sensual Shakespeare

How Far Did He Make It?

Multiple Phone Calls

The Backstory:

I don't know why I find myself always attracting Geminis, but I do. And they are typically intellectual in some aspect with engaging ways of communicating, so it grabs my attention instantly. But it's always a recipe for failure, and every time I tell myself, *'Don't go there,'* I find myself lured into their cute, smooth-talking little webs.

This guy was no different—not to mention, writing was his hobby, so we had that connection in common. He even shared a really inspiring writing challenge that he was working on, and I realized that it was also a great practice for me to get into as an author. So, of course, I wanted to text and talk with this guy; my brain was happily stimulated.

It started out innocent enough, but then he got a little too sexty. I tried to curb it and communicate my sex talk boundaries, clearly letting him know that I was looking for a genuine connection and eventual LTR and that physical intimacy was something I needed to work up to. That included sexting, especially since we had yet to meet. He said he was on the same page, yet the innuendos kept on coming. (You decide if I intended the pun).

At this point, I was getting uncomfortable, and even though I kept deflecting it, he still pushed. In my book, I'm absolutely okay with flirting and being playful—as long as it's natural and respectful and what we both want. But after articulating that his level of expression was crossing a line for me, instead of respecting that, he tried to mansplain to me the difference between intimacy and naughtiness, and that was it for me. I realized that he wanted what I was not going to just hand over to him, and I ended the connection wishing him the best.

Classic Line(s):

"I'd happily barter my cooking skills with your clean-up skills if you'd consider sweetening the pot with some kisses and cuddling."

[Not gonna lie. I love cunning attempts at negotiation.]

"I noticed you were thinking of me so thought I'd say hello."

[He was a clever gent with his lines, so I gotta give him credit for it. It's the writer in him.]

"What I wrote I didn't see as overtly sexual as opposed to passionate. I'm talking intimacy, not necessarily naughty. It could've been taken as romantic and intimate instead of naughty."

[Thanks for mansplaining your still inappropriate comments. Let me womansplain: intimacy isn't given; it's earned.]

Future Character Attributes:

The whole 'writing as a hobby' idea is appealing because most people who enjoy writing actually make a living out of it; this was just his passion. There were lots of great lines he said that I could use, not just flirtatious ones but romantic and sweet ones as well.

Role I Would Assign Him:

I would definitely incorporate his romantic and sensuous words into the prose of a leading man. I could also have a tough character who has a softer side of being a secret writer—a man who is more comfortable expressing himself through the written word when he can't verbalize what he truly feels in his heart.

My Takeaway:

Let down your guard for vulnerability but not for manipulation. When you've clearly communicated your boundaries and they keep being pushed, you're not being (or going to be) respected. Take the hint and go.♥

The Bi-Coastal Dad

─── ❦ ───

How Far Did He Make It?
Phone Call/Canceled Date

The Backstory:

He was a sophisticated house flipper who bought, transformed, and sold homes all over the country, flying back and forth between California and New York often. His job appeared solid, and he was cool to talk to, but he did seem to take the flirting a little too far at times, and I needed to curb it. Plus, it was immature at times, and I wasn't sure this guy was as sophisticated socially as he was professionally.

Since I was in my post-bucket list phase, where I realized I was not going to subject myself to hookups at that point, I wasn't being as flirtatious as I think he wished I could be. I still indulged the innocent flirting, and we had plans to meet up for ice cream, but the plans fell through for him at the last minute. I got the feeling it was because I wasn't giving the right signs that I would actually sleep with him in exchange for the ice cream, and so he disappeared. I went and bought myself ice cream anyway, and it was damn good.

Classic Line(s):

"That's what she said."

[Funny once. Not when repeated multiple times like a toddler.]

"Can I buy you some ice cream and maybe make out with you?"

[Props for the cute come-on. It wasn't going to work, but I did laugh and thought it was original.]

Future Character Attributes:

I dig the potential duplicity of living two lives on two different coasts. Perhaps he was a house flipper or real estate agent in California but a strip club owner in New York. I don't know, but it's kind of cool to think about characters that could have multiple lives. And his pickup line was cute—I might have to use that somewhere.

Role I Would Assign Him:

I think he'd be a great "I want to introduce you to…" character that tries to disrupt the real romance (you know, the best friend secretly in love with her), but once his deceptive lifestyle comes out, she realizes she's meant to be with her bestie all along kind of deal.

My Takeaway:

Get the hint when they are dropping too many flirtatious innuendos. Don't stick around just to be stood up—excuse yourself and move on. ♥

Yabba Dabba Don't

How Far Did He Make It?
One Date

The Backstory:

This is one hot mess of a date story! So first off, his profile was all about not knowing where we intellectual women are and wondering why it is so hard to find stimulating conversation these days. Enter our match chat, and he barely responds with anything of substance. So, I wonder the same thing about men in return, but then I remember sometimes people open up more in person than over chat. We exchanged numbers and text for a bit, then made plans for a date.

We were going to meet up with him in Koreatown, and he surprised me by suggesting a street fair that was around the corner from his house. *'How fun and creative for a first date,'* I thought to myself. Loving events like that in general and envisioning a fun afternoon, I headed on up toward LA, truly excited for this date. That fizzled quickly.

It started off with me not being able to find parking, and when I called him to ask what I should do, he mentioned that he had to take one of his cars to the repair shop, so if I could give him a lift there, I could then park in his normal spot. *Um, okay.* So, I dumbly said to myself, *'Yeah, sure, why not let a complete stranger into my car to take him to his parked car and then follow him to a closed mechanic garage on a random Sunday? How harmful could that possibly be?'*

So, he gets into my car, and he reeks—I mean REEKS—of pot. He wasn't even wearing any cologne or anything to cover it up.

He side-hugs me hello (I'm seated in the car), and then after he gets his car, I proceed to follow the maniac driver to the mechanic, grateful to have been brought up in New York and understanding his Brooklyn-born driving skills—which, might I add, were no doubt worsened by his royal high-ness. Anyway, he then gets back into my car to head back toward his place and the fair to park. We chat a little bit, and he's somewhat cool but not the deep conversationalist I was hoping for.

We walked to the street fair and stayed there for all of 20 minutes. Not kidding. We walked up and down, did nothing but get a cup of corn and some water, and then he said we could eat it in his apartment. I should have declined, but that wouldn't have brought me to the most interesting part of this story. I go upstairs, and smoke is everywhere from cigarettes, weed, and cigars, all three of which he continued to light up and smoke while we ate corn and watched—wait for it—the Flintstones. There was a marathon on. And all I could awkwardly do was watch and pretend to laugh along with him until he kissed me, and I decided I might as well go for it and get something out of this date. He did check off a bucket list item for me.

The television was on in the background the entire time. I can assure you that hearing "Yabba Dabba Do" at a certain peak moment took on a whole new meaning for me, and it's not an experience I will ever forget.

Yes, that really happened.

And so after that humorous disaster, I sped my way back home but not before unmatching and telling myself how lucky I was not to have been a victim on the news. Looking back on all the risks I took, I really should not have put myself in the precarious situation I did. I'm grateful it all turned out okay, but I won't ever do something like that again. On the other hand, I have a great date story to laugh about with my girlfriends. Yabba Dabba Doooooooo!

Classic Line(s):

"Is there a woman out there who knows how to hold a conversation?"

[About what? Hanna-Barbera cartoons?]

"Yo, let's get some corn. Want some?"

[What a generous guy. We got to share a cup of coquita corn—but I got my own bottle of water, so there's that.]

Future Character Attributes:

I don't know. He was quite a character. Where would I begin? His chivalry? Nope. He didn't even offer me anything to smoke while he did it, so forget manners. His maturity? Nope. Didn't exist. I feel like all of the debacle surrounding the date is good stuff, like if I wrote a comedy, I could work with a few things that went on in the apartment during our date. But as for character attributes? I'm coming up short.

Role I Would Assign Him:

He doesn't exactly inspire a character as much as a funny scene, but we'll see. I may have yet to turn this experience into something author-worthy. Stay tuned.

My Takeaway:

Don't go to some random stranger's house in Koreatown, for goodness' sake. That had potential rape and murder written all over it. I am lucky he was just high and not homicidal. ♥

Mr. Nice Guy

How Far Did He Make It?

Two Dates

The Backstory:

Sometimes we meet people who we just aren't attracted to but who are interesting, nonetheless. When I say this was a nice guy, I mean genuinely, sincerely nice. He was a dad to a little girl, and it showed in the way he had the ultimate respect in every conversation we had. He was a slow mover, much slower than I was used to, but I liked the change of pace and consciously chose to let it ride. It took over a month of talking and my suggestion to exchange numbers for it to move forward off the app, then another few weeks until it finally progressed to a dinner date.

He wasn't what I expected, but he was a great conversationalist. We talked for hours about our businesses and professional life and hobbies, and I did get the vibe that he'd be really cool to continue getting to know. After we had worn out our welcome at the restaurant, he asked me if I wanted to do something else but offered no suggestions, and I didn't have any either. Since it was the area he lived in, I let him take the lead, but he ended up just walking me to my car without even a kiss goodnight.

I didn't want that to bother me; I wanted that to be a good thing, I told myself. Here was a man interested in conversation and getting to know me instead of jumping into my pants. He had a good job, was independent, kind, and a good dad. So, I gave it one more shot for a second date.

We ended up going to a movie, which didn't lend itself to much talking or getting to know each other further, and it ultimately felt awkward as neither of us made a romantic move. Sensing this wasn't what either of us was looking for, I communicated that I didn't think this wasn't the right fit for us. Then, as mature adults, we wished each other well and decided we could remain friendly and chat from time to time.

I did hear a hello from him recently, but it never materialized beyond that, but it was nice to know someone still thought of me. It was quite refreshing, actually.

Classic Line(s):

"I'm ready to wave the white flag. I can't seem to meet an honest woman here."

[Um, hello? You are literally talking to one.]

"Thank you for being honest and not doing the ghost thing. If you ever want to get together again, would love to see you again."

[Now there is a kind gentleman if I ever met one.]

Future Character Attributes:

He is the all-around good guy that most women look for in a man. All of his maturity and stability, from professional to emotional, would create a truly solid foundation for a good male character.

Role I Would Assign Him:

Add in some romantic sex appeal, and I think he'd be a really worthy lead for a woman who is perhaps the erratic one and could use the love of a grounded man.

My Takeaway:

Even though I might not have physical chemistry with every guy I meet, I sure do enjoy meeting people who I can have interesting conversations with, and that experience can be just as pleasant as a romantic date.🖤

TEXTS YOU SHOULDN'T READ INTO AS "MEANINGFUL" OR "HEARFELT"

*Actual screenshots of texts written to me in between verbally declaring how "connected" we are on multiple levels.

Ok signing off it's such a tease chatting with you but not having you here... Hrummph! 😒

And stop being so goddamn magical and fun to talk to! 😊

Glad to hear it!The beauty of your prose is bested only by that of your soul 😊 My rocketship is also fine, but tiring of training missions 😒

Have an equally intergalactically stellar day 😊

Wow on so many levels!! I literally feel every word, and I mean FEEL... It's like you took a sensory recording of our every interaction and played it back in blissful sorround... I am awed, honored... and incredibly turned on... By your words, by your soul... By you 😊

Thank you so much for sharing, you just made my... heart shine 🖤

And so the 🦋 😊 blinked, uncertain if this new world revealed was truly the paradise that it seemed... slowly, her wings unfurled, revealing her beautiful, bold explosion of technicolor, patterned perfection in all its glory. Prince ▓▓▓▓ smiled knowingly, his garden state of heart and mind flourishing wildly with every infatuatingly elegant flutter. 😊

Artwork Credit: Andrei Rybalko/Depositphotos.com

The Intergalactic Blindside

How Far Did He Make It?

Almost Relationship

The Backstory:

This man was dear to me, and I debated between sharing this story or letting it be. Ultimately, I decided to share it because it was an important part of my journey, but out of respect, I am taking a lot of care to treat this experience with as much tenderness as I can while also being true to my feelings.

He was outside of my typical type, which tends to be this bad-boy-never-turned-good, like in romance novels. Instead, he was kind, emotionally intelligent, consistent, non-toxic, and adorably dorky. Our intellectual compatibility was off the charts. I'm not a big movie person, but I knew every movie reference he made. Our sense of humor was identical—sharp, witty, and quick.

I had undoubtedly met my mental match. That's how our connection started, though he was hesitant at first because of our distance. We decided to take the chance and meet up anyway, even if it meant we'd just end up friends.

Our first date was such a pleasant surprise. He put in the effort to make it special, and we went to an outdoor classical concert. It was romantic, comfortable, and effortless. Beforehand, we had talked for quite a while and found so much in common that it was unreal. Not only was the mental connection there, but there was this emotional connection that was unlike any I had ever experienced, and we were also spiritually aligned. We just seemed to get each other. Fast forward to the end of the evening, and we found that we also had physical chemistry. It seemed like, on every level, we were connected, and it surprised both of us.

Well, this was during a summer when we both had exciting travel plans, and we wouldn't get to a second date for another month. So, I didn't stress about it. I was going to let it unfold... and it did. We couldn't stop texting each other and sharing our pictures and experiences. And it wasn't over the top, either. It was a natural communication that developed between us.

He'd play piano for me and write this beautiful prose that made me feel special, and I'd write him sweet sentiments in return. He actually read an important book of mine and took the time to read other stories I wrote, and that meant the world to me. We'd talk on the phone and share more and more about ourselves, creating this foundational bond in a really cool way. So by the time we did get to the second date, it felt further along than that, and it was easy to spend the whole day getting to know each other even better when we did meet up.

The third date ended up being my birthday weekend, and all I will say is that I have never been treated so well in my entire life. Uncomfortably spoiled, but I accepted it because I realized I deserved it. But it was so much more than him paying for things; he gave me the most thoughtful gifts a man has ever given me, and I couldn't have imagined a better person to spend that time with. He kept commenting on how we connected on so many levels and asking if this—if *I*—was real. I didn't expect to feel so strongly safe, open, trusting, and comfortable with someone so quickly, and I was glad that I looked beyond his not being my normal type because what we were building was everything I had ever wanted.

And I had the impression that he felt the same based on his words and actions. Until he asked me a seemingly benign question, and it all unraveled because we actually were not on the same page. Even though he exhibited every possible sign that we were moving toward something special, he revealed that he wasn't looking for a relationship and just wanted something casual. Not that he wanted to be promiscuous, but he wanted to explore his options still.

It hit me like a ton of bricks. I genuinely didn't see that coming. And it wasn't like I was in a rush to get to a serious commitment, but once he opened the conversation up, I was honest about what I was looking for… and I was blindsided to find out after everything he said, did, and shared that we weren't at least headed that way.

Even so, we talked it through like emotionally mature adults and ultimately decided that I deserved a commitment and he deserved to explore, and neither of us should compromise what felt right to us. It hurt like hell, but only a few days after that magical birthday weekend, our "relationship" abruptly ended, and we went our separate ways, wondering if we were making the right choice or if perhaps one day we could be friends. He seemed on the fence about whether to give us a fair chance or not, so I had a little hope that maybe things could be different one day. I thought some time apart would bring clarity, so we let each other go with a lot of understanding and respect.

Well, fast forward to only 45 days later: I reach out to say hello, only to find out he met someone and was happily in a relationship. Now, I don't begrudge anyone happiness, and I do wish him and his partner all the best, but the speed at which he went from not wanting a relationship at all to being in one so soon after we parted left my heart a bit jaded about whether

I could believe anyone's intentions ever again. The way this imploded and ended up left me a bit disheartened and closed off because I truly thought we had something real. Clearly, I was way off base.

I never saw it coming, and it was one of the toughest rejections of my life because I truly felt misled.

Classic Line(s):

"Our horoscope said we'd have great conversation but ultimately just be friends."

[Damn, I love me some good, witty verbal swordplay. Bring it, Lancelot.]

"I closed off the rest of the world, but for some reason, your channel remains open."

[He was on a solitary vacation but was keeping in touch and sharing his experience with me every step of the way.]

"Who are you? Are you even real? You are unlike any woman I've ever met before."

[He asked me this multiple times.]

"I literally feel every word, and I mean FEEL. I am awed and honored by your words, by your soul... by YOU. You just made my heart shine."

[One of many heartfelt responses he shared along the way.]

"In the interest of deepening our relationship, I want to share this with you. To build a meaningful connection. And I know you out of anyone will be able to understand what I've gone through."

[Then he shared something very vulnerable with me—yet he wanted just casual all along? #mixedsignals]

Future Character Attributes:

There was so much of his persona that I adored. His wit was unparalleled, and his intellectual depth was swoon-worthy for a sapiosexual like me—and probably my readers. He also had this softness, a gentleness in his voice and touch that was in stark contrast to his brilliant bantering abilities, and I think he does make for pretty great character material.

Role I Would Assign Him:

Definitely some kind of leading man… without the emotional flip-flop.

My Takeaway:

I certainly learned a lot from this man… one of which was a reawakening to certain life passions that had been dormant, such as my writing and acting. He wasn't just a romantic interest but a friend, a coach, and an inspiration—and I will carry all the lessons he taught me in my heart. And I realized how very much I love naturally romantic men who know how to make me feel special through words and thoughtful gestures. It was really nice to have that experience, however brief it lasted.

But in the end, I can't assume anything—words and actions don't always convey a man's actual truth. Conversations are critical at a certain point *before* you go and start giving your heart away.♥

Surprise! I'm Married

How Far Did He Make It?

Phone Call/Canceled Date

The Backstory:

His profile told me more about him than his numerous texts. First, he was looking for a connection. Then he was looking for something casual, not serious. Then, he revealed on the app that he was in an open marriage. None of which had come out while texting and making plans to meet up for a date. I think him being married was something he should have started out with, don't you? And… it would have been easy for him to tell me directly as he had multiple conversations and opportunities during which to share that critical piece of information.

Before that, however, I was intrigued. Another writer who was good with words captured my attention right off the bat. It was a quick connection, and we planned to meet for dinner and live music, but he couldn't make it because of having to travel back east to get his dad. His poor dad had Alzheimer's, and he was going to bring him back to California, where he could help be his caretaker, which seemed really nice of him. So, we agreed to meet up the next week instead before I was to travel for summer vacation. I ended up being the one asking for a postponement since I was overwhelmed with getting things set for the trip, and he agreed it could wait until I got back.

We continued to text while I was away, and he followed me on IG—but his profile was a little on the disturbing side. Between that and then seeing his updated open marriage info in his profile, I shut that shit down immediately. I don't need a shady married man in my life when I'm looking for my own happily ever after. No, thank you. Next!

Classic Line(s):

"I love that you are a sapiosexual. Nothing better than being with someone who gets how words are hot."

[Maybe I shouldn't give away that hint so early in the game and save myself some potential manipulation.]

"How do you feel about naughty pics?"

[Well, at least he respectfully asked before sending them unsolicited. And he got points for respecting my view and being cool about my no thanks.]

Future Character Attributes:

I liked the caregiving part of him—if that was even actually a real scenario: his flying back east to pack up his dad and bring him home to a facility closer to him where he could take better care of him. It's very humanitarian and warm.

Role I Would Assign Him:

I could use the caregiving arrangement for an interesting story about a woman who meets a man who is a parental caregiver and see a love story play out between them—without the surprise open marriage part, of course. I can see it almost like they both meet in the facility, facing the same fate, and working through it together serendipitously.

My Takeaway:

Remember that anyone, at any time, can have a background they are hiding from you. Be a little more discerning in connections from certain player-oriented sites.♥

A Dory of a Dom

♥

How Far Did He Make It?

One Date

The Backstory:

Oh, Dory. When do I begin? We moved fast from app texting to calling because he hates chats and believes in developing relationships through phone conversations and in person. I was down with that because I was so tired of all of the failing dates and endless texting that got me nowhere. I found him to be rather interesting.

He owned two businesses, one of which was in transportation, and it clearly afforded him quite the affluential lifestyle. He talked endlessly about the expensive renovations he was making to his house, indoor hot tub, and outdoor swimming pool, and it all sounded so luxurious. He mentioned liking a certain kind of shoes on women, and when I said I didn't own them, he said he'd just buy them for me, that he'd buy me whatever I wanted. He wanted to take care of me.

I will admit, for a split second, that sounded oh-so-appealing—but I knew that there would be something more to it, and I'm not the kind of girl who just likes guys to spend money on her. A nice dinner, yes. Clothes, purses, shoes, vacations? I'm no one's sugar baby, and it makes me super uncomfortable to think of accepting that level of spoiling.

But aside from that, I really felt like we connected in general, so I put that uncomfortableness to the side and decided to just enjoy getting to know him.

Now you would think that after talking about all his money and how he wants to spoil me that I'd be in for a halfway decent dinner at least. Yeah, no. I arrived at our meeting spot—an outdoor mall—and he didn't have anything planned. He randomly looked around for a quick-service burger joint because he just wanted to eat and hang back out in his limo (we went on a date while he was waiting for a client to be done with their concert. Um, cool, right?).

While we were talking during dinner, I found him to be pushy with the waiter and quite repetitive, as if he wasn't even listening to a word I said. In fact, he asked me what I was doing the rest of the weekend, and not even five minutes after I told him, he asked me the same question. When I reminded him, that's when he told me that he had short-term memory loss from an accident. And it made a lot of sense, given how he kept telling me the same things over and over about his house and business, so he really was like Dory.

I just kept swimming.

Anyway, we wrapped dinner up quickly and headed out to the limo to hang out, which I have to say was pretty interesting. We chillaxed and chatted some more, and then he kissed me, and damn! That man could kiss. I'd say he tied for ultimate kisser in this book with the real estate workaholic. Seriously, if it wasn't for the fact that he shared certain S&M sexual expectations, had memory loss, and had an unfortunate limpness, I could have enjoyed being spoiled in more ways than one with this guy.

But he was super respectful when I turned down his invitation to be his future sub, so he wasn't a bad guy. Just not aligned with the personal romance novel I'm trying to write for myself.

Classic Line(s):

"I think an independent, alpha woman makes the perfect sub."
[Not this one, but thank you for honoring who I am.]

"You don't have that? Okay, I'll just buy you one."
[I was soooo tempted to stick this one out for kicks…]

Future Character Attributes:

He definitely had mad kissing skills, which will go into the description of a bedroom scene with a very lucky leading lady in one of my books somewhere. Plus, I liked the whole limo thing and think that would make for a fun scene.

Role I Would Assign Him:

He'll be worked into a main character somehow—probably used as a blend with many of these other men I encountered to create one extraordinary lead of all of their best qualities. If I wanted to venture into a dom/sub kind of romance, he did explain a lot of things to me I could use.

My Takeaway:

Good kissers can be found in the most unexpected places. ♥

The English Teacher

---❦---

How Far Did He Make It?
A Few Dates

The Backstory:

This guy was as genuine as they come. Honest, upfront, sweet—he really was an all-around decent guy. He was looking for a relationship, was emotionally and financially stable, smart and quick-witted, and a poet! He was published with a deep appreciation for words and how they can evoke strong emotions in another. Communication was big for him—I always knew where I stood, never wondered if I'd hear from him, and he was happy to make plans and stick to them. It was so easy to go on multiple dates with him.

The first date was super fun and spontaneous—we ended up at a bar where we met a younger married couple (the wife whom I befriended and completely adore), and then together, we went to their friend's live music performance. It was romantic and fun. We clicked right away, both with laughter and chemistry. It tops the charts as one of my all-time, best-ever first dates. It had it all: great food and drinks, music, conversation, laughter, spontaneity, romance… Literally every box checked.

We ended up going on a second date only a few days later for brunch, where we talked more deeply about dating—our crazy experiences, our perspectives as a man and woman in these scenarios, and how difficult it was to find that dating balance without forgetting who we are (we both shared the same concern about our writing falling by the wayside if we get too caught up in a relationship yet we were both seeking one). Though I will admit, I wasn't feeling the pull as strongly on date two as that first evening. But I stuck it out.

We ended up meeting up for a third date, but things took an unexpected turn that neither of us was ready for. For me, something was missing from our connection... and it wasn't that it was him per se as much as I realized my heart wasn't as ready as I thought it was for something new. I was still freshly hurt by another man, and I had no business jumping into something else yet. I had some more soul-searching to do when it came to what I wanted from dating and/or relationships.

He also realized at that moment that he wasn't as ready either—and what happened after was a most beautiful, honest, open-hearted conversation between the two of us. We were safely vulnerable with how we were feeling and how we both needed some extra healing in our own way. I cannot express how genuinely freeing it was to just straight out, on the spot, have an honest talk instead of running and hiding and hoping not to hurt someone else while hurting them, nonetheless.

Instead, we both walked away happy, with mad respect and fondness for each other, and no hard feelings. It was a very positive experience in honesty, emotional maturity, and communication—and I can say with all certainty that I will never settle for less than that kind of communication standard in future relationships.

I learned so much from him and appreciated him in my life. I might have been shown this experience to understand the other perspective—how it feels from a man's point of view. It's only going to make me a better person by understanding how I can respond, act, and be in nurturing connections. Love is hard, but vulnerability doesn't have to be.

Classic Line(s):

"Hope he gives you a good rating."

[LOL. After I mentioned I had to go play "Mom Uber" for my son and his friends.]

"Long texts are my jam. Bring it on."

[Finally, someone who can appreciate my need for written verbosity at times.]

"Everything you do is cute. All these things that you think are weird about you are what I find absolutely adorable."

[So damn sweet.]

Future Character Attributes:

His sense of humor was off the charts and had me laughing the whole time. And yet he also had this deeply serious side to him that was open-hearted and endearing. He wasn't afraid to be intimate with his feelings, and he knew the right time to be sensitive and the right time to be funny. I did also enjoy the poet in him and how romantically expressive he was.

Role I Would Assign Him:

A really good leading man with all the qualities of a well-rounded love interest.

My Takeaway:

I took away so much information about how women are online and in dating, and it was pretty appalling to hear some of his stories. I also came to understand men in general, as he'd share what goes on in the male psyche in different scenarios. It really is true that if they are interested, you will be pursued, and if not, hang it up because it's no use pursuing a ghost.

But my most important takeaway was how communication really is key—just talk about it. No matter how difficult you think it might be to say. It is better to say the hard truths with kindness and understanding as you feel them than hide them under the selfish guise of "protecting" another's feelings. It hurt a lot less to be real than to be diplomatic, and a genuine hug goodbye is worth more than a passive-aggressive misunderstanding could ever be.♥

Notable Mentions

A REFRESHINGLY UPFRONT PROFILE THAT I PASSED ON... BUT RESPECTED FOR ITS BRUTAL HONESTY

About me

In search of meaningless ongoing fucking relationship.

I am a chivalrous gentleman.

Drummer that will rock you.

If you don't shave your cookie, swipe left.

He Said What?!?

This section is dedicated to those who didn't get very far, but damn, did some of their one-liners warrant acknowledgment in a book about bumbling idiots—I mean, date potentials. In fact, most of these were their final lines before I unmatched but not before committing them to memory or paper.

Others were most definitely cute or witty enough to engage a little bit longer until the vibe wasn't there or a ghost appeared... Mad props to those who were unique and clever!

Enjoy!

Not-So-Subtle Sugar Baby:

"So, where are we going with our money...uh, *your* money? LOL"

Dog Daddy:

"Okay, Princess. You can call me Papi."

Boy Toy:

"I'm into older, mature women who know what they want. The sex is gonna be great!"

Hike That Never Happened:

"Sorry I'm so flaky. When are we supposed to do that again?"

Insulting Complimenter:

"I don't usually date heavy girls, but it's okay. I really like you anyway."

Tattoo Enthusiast:

"We could connect someplace else if you'd like."

Storyteller:

"I'm an astrophysicist and forensic psychologist on the side. And I'm currently training for the Olympics for table tennis... Just joking. I just cook, eat, and ride my skateboard."

Polite Cowboy:

"You seem so intelligent. Not sure I can hang like that. I'm not so smart."

Aviation Cuddler:

"Just landed. If only my reach were a little bit longer, I'd wake you up, give you a hug, and then cuddle you. Wink."

Potential Serial Killer:

"We're going up to San Francisco tonight to celebrate the wrap of my movie. It's 10 of us going on my plane. You should come!"

Eye-Rolling Unoriginality:

"Are you tired from running through my thoughts all day?"

Fetish Freak:

"How do you feel about me making love to your feet?"

Sex Negotiator:

"How about... sex whenever it happens, no boundaries or expectations. Let's just enjoy each other."

Pre-Exchange Warner:

"Sure, sweetheart, but only if you share pictures with me."

Super Christian:

"I'm not telling you my sign. I don't believe that planetary distances do anything to help humanity. Only God and His servants do."

Scorpio Hottie:

"Let's chat offline. Here's my number. What kind of greeting would you like?"

Bubba Gump:

"But I have to work. I don't have any shrimping boats."

Potential Client:

"Also, what's your opinion on my bio? How can I edit it to sound better and get more matches?"

Witty Responder:

"My sign? Lately, with my dating luck, I think my sign is STOP. LOL."

Overeager Connector:

"When you are traveling, think of me so that I can feel like I am there with you."

Scammer Alert:

"Don't you like texting? I don't like to call in a hurry. We can use wassup."

Dear Bumbling Boy...

Refreshing Dawn Dater:

"I want to see comfy clothes, no makeup, and hair pulled back. Bring the big smile."

Busted Me Juggling:

"I think we've had this conversation before. I'm having déjà vu."

Wrong Number Corrected:

"Omg. I was whispering sweet nothings into someone else's phone?"

Lovebomber:

"You're so sweet, Jenny. I think I'm in love with you."

Big Man On The Job:

"I tell big companies what to do. Does that qualify?"

Bubba Gump Part 2:

"I just envision Forrest Gump yelling, Jenny, I got you an ice cream."

Wishful Thinker:

"We should figure out an evening or afternoon to have a drink. Who knows, we might drink enough to make some bad decisions."

The Massive Bodybuilder:

"That's not my real name. You can call me B*** from Brooklyn, aka the Black Hulk."

Co-Dependent Alcoholic:

"Just got back from an A.A. meeting. Why aren't you answering my video call? Are you hiding something?"

The Charmer:

"My travel list… I guess *[Jenny's hometown]* just got put at the top of the list."

The Random Interviewer:

"Are you always late? Do you have a Disney pass? Are you religious?"

Groupie Seeker:

"Fan me on ReverbNation… Easier for you to hear my music and then me explain it."

Dirty Chef:

"Just don't come around in that pig costume or I might be tempted to cook you like bacon and eat you." ♥

Epilogue:
The One Who Made it to My Heart

I can't write a book about online dating without acknowledging one of my definitive "success stories." But that is all I will do: acknowledge him.

I will not expose or disrespect him in any way because I cared about him, and he still means something to me. And while this relationship ultimately didn't work out, I will give this special man nothing but gratitude for the profound lessons he taught me.

We were meant to cross paths, and the only personal information I will share about him is a memorable quote from when we first met; something he said that was genuine as he looked into my eyes with instant affection. It captured my heart when he said it because I felt the same exact thing at that moment: kismet undoubtedly brought us together for a reason.

"Are you sure we've never met before? I feel like I've known you forever."

Okay, I'll share one more, just because it made me feel so incredibly adored. It was one of the sweetest, most random messages I received in the middle of the workday with no hidden agenda, come-on, or kiss-up intended.

"I love when I lay in your lap, and you look at me with your beautiful blue eyes."

All the other pages of men before and after this—the bumblers with the bad pickup lines, the boundary crossers, the scammers and narcissists, the sexual predators, and so on—were all worth culling through to get to this man and this experience.

Dear Bumbling Boy...

Two years ago, I had never tried giving online dating a chance. I'd make a profile and talk to a few guys, but nothing materialized, and I just wasn't into it. I was adamant about never meeting a guy this way; it wasn't for me. I couldn't possibly connect with anyone online because it's all about the in-person energy vibe for me.

And so, for many years, I refused to consider online dating as an option, holding out for that "inevitable" meet-cute that I was destined to have. Ask me how many dates I went on during that very long dry spell, thanks to my stubbornness.

But as a dear friend of mine pointed out to me, that's not how it works these days. Sure, the in-person serendipitous type of connection still happens, and I'm sure there are traditional love stories from co-workers who fell in love or from couples who met through mutual interest groups, through friends, or even through random encounters in the Walmart pet food aisle. However, she was right; this, unfortunately, is where it is at if I truly was serious about meeting someone or even just having the dating experience.

Her advice also came with a realistic warning: you might have to go through 80 bad eggs to find one worth even going on a date with. Clearly, I've been through some bad eggs, and no doubt, I've appeared as a bad egg myself. It's all part of this process.

So I embarked on this journey, and it was messy. *I* was messy. I teetered between a commitment to being vulnerably open and fulfilling self-sabotaging, self-doubt tendencies with a touch of shame. I entered this wanting a long-term relationship but then, after being hurt, went on a binger of not caring if they were genuine or not. I didn't believe that there were all that many men out there looking for something real, so I played the dating game.

And I hated it. I can't do the juggling thing, and I don't want to. But that was another lesson I needed to learn as I experienced what it was like trying to remember who was who when we'd have conversations or meet. It felt inauthentic of me, and after indulging in some questionable (for me) behavior, I got tired of being disrespected and disrespecting myself and drew hard lines.

I knew what I was willing to accept and not accept. I unmatched quicker when I saw the warning signs or felt a lack of alignment instead of holding on to the possibility of wasted time. I looked for a genuine connection, and while some started out that way and revealed different colors later, I still was proud that I held my ground when things no longer aligned.

At the end of the day, I became clear on who, how, and what terms I was willing to enter into as a result of a match. It definitely narrowed down options, but that's exactly how it needed to be for me to be led to the right kinds of matches.

What I will say, however, is that I am glad I finally took that risk. I removed the "never" block and opened myself up to whatever the dating experience could teach me. I am even grateful that I went through this process more than once and subjected myself to different kinds of people and conversations.

To be honest, I joke about how bad these "characters" were, but I actually came away with some interesting new knowledge from a bunch of these conversations and connections.

One guy recommended a book that blew my mind. Another mentioned how he likes to ride upstate to an adorable little town, which I ended up going to myself and falling in love with. Another writer inspired a writing challenge that pushed me to grow my skills. One man and I had a four-hour conversation that led to mutual breakthroughs in the way we approached our businesses.

I gleaned so much information on how men approach the dating process, why they do things in certain ways, and how they themselves are treated. Yet another man inadvertently steered me toward writing this book based on my dating research.

Not everything was for naught. It taught me the nuances of interacting with men: how to discern the genuine from the hit-it-and-quit-it; how to balance my alpha personality with my wanting-to-be-expressed femininity while honoring their innate, non-toxic masculinity; and how to be uniquely interesting enough to capture their attention (spoiler alert: by being authentically me).

It taught me a lot about myself: my expectations, my approach, and my readiness at different stages of the process.

It also taught me how to communicate better; how to not be so rigid or scared in taking a next step; and how to open my mind up to learning about the beauty of different people who don't always fit the mold we envision for ourselves.

All of these different men showed me what was possible in a relationship. I wouldn't have been able to learn more about myself had I not gone through these experiences that taught me what I clearly wanted—and what I deserved.

Most importantly, my journey brought me to this significant man, who helped to heal, challenge, and strengthen my heart and ability to love and trust. It brought me to someone who taught me that good people exist and that not everyone is a narcissist out to abuse me. With him, I experienced kindness, protection, attentiveness, and a healthy spark that could have led to long-term success if only we were meant for each other.

He also gratefully taught me how not to settle for certain behaviors and patterns. I found myself repeating a cycle and learned so much about breaking it, honoring myself, trying on new ways of responding, and ultimately, choosing self-love. I have laughed, learned, cried, agonized, and opened up because of him, and I'd like to think that it all made me a stronger, wiser, better woman at the end of the day.

Who knows where life will bring any of us next. Endings are not always gruesome, and happy endings are not always predictable or timely.

I haven't given up just yet. Though the journey through countless bumbling boys continues, I still hold out faith that I will ultimately find the right man in harmony with my heart. One day.♥

Just One More...

Intro

speechless...and I'm genuinely interested in you, and a little afraid at how you jump-started the beat of my heart just now, and it gave me an urgent craving that worried me that you might be able to hypnotize me willingly with your intelligence and your passion and your allure. 🐾🖤⚓

To be quite frank, you have my strong attention, and I would like to move this forward with you at once 🌊

After Phone Convo

So tell me honestly because I respect it: I want your gut feeling walking away from our first conversation people know in their heart sometimes it takes a little longer but you'll know when your heart so I'm asking you to tell me if you have a gut feeling about me and if it's to draw closer or to part respectfully?

10 More Min After Phone Convo

If you're excited and can't wait to talk to me again please tell me that if it's anything else then tell me

Because I think I'll take a pass if it's the latter

After My Patiently Crafted Response

I'm very vibe sensitive I could tell we weren't totally hitting it off and we were looking for different things I trust my gut if you weren't eager to hear back from me then it wasn't natural and that's what I'm looking for among other things I just know we aren't a fit and I hope you have a great night though thank you for your time you're a very nice lady and I hope you have a great Thanksgiving as well 🙏

The End.

Acknowledgments

This was such a fun book to write, and it wouldn't have happened if it weren't for several of my girlfriends encouraging me to share some of my craziest stories with the world. Those friends who were single also inspired a lot of introductory insight as we shared horror stories and mishaps.

But it wasn't just their "how fun would it be to write that book" kind of encouragement that I appreciated, but the steady, unwavering support they gave me as I went through this process.

I'm not sure I would have survived this online dating journey without multiple warning reminders, check-in calls, bail-me-out calls, location sharing, background checks, and (eventually heeded) sage advice.

Laura, Kristen, Pam, Minzi, Kimberly, Brenna, and Molly—thanks for keeping me grounded while non-judgmentally supporting all my bad decisions. A girl couldn't ask for a better cheerleading squad. Who needs a man when I have your unconditional love?

I am also deeply appreciative of my advanced readers, especially Hilary Ritter (Young), who didn't hesitate for a second to support my work. Her kindness overwhelmed me—and her introduction? Her generosity and insight truly touched me.

As a side note: I loved her astrology dating site and wish it still existed, as back then, I wasn't ready to actually pay online dating any mind. I wonder how different life would have been had I taken more chances years ago. But her success has inspired me to keep going—there is a prince out there waiting for me.

I also have to thank my incredible editor/proofreader, Abby, for making sure my t's and i's were in proper working order and for her always spot-on feedback.

An anonymous shout-out to another friend, RB, for the invaluable insight that led to the creative, sassy reels all over my social media. One Zoom call is all it sometimes takes for inspiration to hit, and yes, AI can be funnier than voiceovers.

Much love and thanks as always to my family for loving me just the way that I am. And sorry in advance to my mom, who will probably worry about me ten times more now after reading this. (Just know my crew has my back and won't let anything bad happen to me).

Most importantly, thank you to all the men who have entered my life in any capacity. I may have made humorous jokes at your expense, but I have a lot of gratitude for your time, for your authentic sharing, and for the lessons you taught me. You made me strive to be a better woman, and I thank you for that.

May we all find what we are looking for in life and love.♥

Other Books by Jenny Dee

The Lost Heritage Trilogy
Call of the Celts
A Tuscan Treasure
The Catalan Key

Autobiographical Memoirs
Butterfly Travels
Butterfly Travels 2

Independent Titles
Beat Me With Your Words
A Cali Christmas

The Cosmic Kids Club Series
Meet the Z Team
Planet Personalities
Stars Live in Houses, Too
Cosmic Kids Astrology
Numerology for Kids

About Jenny Dee

An avid writer since childhood, my career in professional writing anchored my passion and encouraged my dream to become an author—my first book, *Butterfly Travels,* was published in 2014. Five years later, my children joined me in both my physical and literary journeys, sharing our family adventures with the world through *Butterfly Travels 2.*

I have since released a children's astrology and numerology book series (co-authored with my dear friend, Stephanie Foley), as well as an empowered women's trilogy, a traditional holiday romance, and a poignant fictional abuse novel written to enlighten, relate to, and empower survivors to thrive.

I've never been a "one size fits all" type of girl. I like to connect to all kinds of people and share my stories and experiences in hopes that they touch a life. I don't ever want my inspiration to be limited to a single genre, so it is with a great love for writing that I offer a multitude of styles to strike your fancy, from travel memoirs and children's books to women's literature and steamy romance.

To learn more about me or to subscribe to my publications, you can find me at <u>www. jennydeeauthor.com</u> or simply scan this QR code.

~ Find Yourself in a Character ~

www.ingramcontent.com/pod-product-compliance
Lightning Source LLC
Chambersburg PA
CBHW060504280326
41933CB00014B/2860